Who Wants to Be a
Aberdonian?

Fa Wints tae Be un
Aiburdonian?

Patricia Marshall

BLACK & WHITE PUBLISHING

Dedicated to Poppy, an affa fine
wee Aiburdonian

First published 2003
by Black & White Publishing
99 Giles Street, Edinburgh EH6 6BZ

ISBN 1902927 94X

A CIP catalogue record for this book is available
from The British Library

Cover design by McCusker Graphic Media

Printed and bound by Nørhaven Paperback A/S,
Viborg Denmark

CONTENTS

INTRODUCTION

With their widely acknowledged reputation for meanness, you may well ask, 'Who wants to be an Aberdonian?' After all, it's not exactly a quality to aspire to, is it? There are two famous photos that supposedly encapsulate the spirit of Aberdonians. One of them shows the streets of the city deserted and, below it, the caption reads, 'Aberdeen on a street collection day for charity'. In the other, the streets are thronged with folk and the caption reads, 'Aberdeen on a house-to-house collection day for charity'. But anyone who has ever spent any length of time in the city will have experienced the generosity of the city's people – and not just in financial terms – and will know that their reputation for meanness couldn't be further from the truth.

So how did Aberdonians come to be thought of as being stingier than your average Scot? The story goes that it was actually due to flamboyant overspending! In a 'Fa's like us?' spirit that, I suspect, has a lot in common with the building of Scotland's new parliament, the construction of the city-centre viaducts and buildings cost an absolute fortune. The council's overspend took its toll and the city was severely strapped for cash. Bankruptcy beckoned and so the civil purse strings had to be drawn in tight so that spending council money became as rare as the Pittodrie board giving the manager enough money to buy a decent player. The result was that, when visiting dignitaries came to the city, they were dismayed by the lack of hospitality on offer. Off they went back home, mumping on about no civic receptions, no fancy lunches, no dinners comprising more courses than a person has fingers. This happened at the time when the music halls were at the height of their popularity and it wasn't long before the stand-up comedians of the day began incorporating these tales of Aberdeen's lack of cash into their acts. And so the myth – for, as we all know, it is a myth – of Aberdonians being tight-fisted was born.

But it's not just others who enjoy a good laugh at our citizens' being branded penny-pinching skinflints. Aberdonians are at the front of the queue to exploit this reputation and use it to laugh at this caricature of themselves. This joy in self-mockery continues today and is possibly most evident in the songs and chants you can hear at Pittodrie. For example, when faced with an opposition's taunt of 'Sheep-shagging b*****ds, you're only sheep-shagging b*****ds!', do Dons fans care? Not only do they not care, they revel in being the 'butt' of the joke and join in, changing *you're* to *we're* and extending the first syllable to a long bleating noise!

So, if the stereotyped reputation for meanness is misplaced, what are Aberdeen folk really like? Tackle this quiz and you'll find them to be funny – Harry Gordon, the Scotland the What? team – inventive – Sir David Gill, Robert Davidson – talented – Archibald Simpson, Annie Lennox – caring – Bishop Elphinstone, Mary Slessor – great sports people – Denis Law, David Wilkie – in fact, just the best folk you could ever hope to meet!

I've done my best to ensure that all the questions and answers are accurate. However, if there are any errors, I alone am responsible for them. I hope you enjoy the quiz and that you find at least some of the information in the book interesting. Good luck!

Patricia

THE QUESTIONS

'The Silver City with the Golden Sands'

A slogan first coined between the world wars to tempt tourists to our lovely city.

1

Geography
Far uboot's 'at?

We'll start with a quick romp through the byways, parks, gardens, churches, pubs and other landmarks that make Aberdeen one of the most attractive cities in the UK.

1 How many Aberdeens are there in the world?

a	Just over 20	b	Just over 50
c	Just over 30	d	Just over 40

2 What is the name of the Granite City's huge quarry?

a	Rubislaw	b	Rosemount
c	Westburn	d	Hamilton

3 And what's the huge gothic granite building in the city centre called?

a	St Nicholas House	b	The Bon-Accord Centre
c	Marischal College	d	The Student Union

4 Near the Castlegate, there's a narrow lane called Lodge Walk. How did this wee street get its name?

a	It led to a men's lodging house	b	It led to Mrs Lodge's guest house
c	It led to the back entrance of a hotel where Masonic meetings were held	d	It led to the Marischal College porter's lodge

5 What's the local name for the road junction at the top of George Street?

a	Calsayseat Bifurcation	b	Kitty Corner
c	Split-the-Win'	d	Powis Pairtin'

6 Whose statue stands across the road from His Majesty's Theatre?

a	Robert Burns's	b	Prince Albert's
c	Robert the Bruce's	d	William Wallace's

7 And whose statue sits on the grassy area just behind this?

a	Queen Victoria's	b	Prince Albert's
c	Edward VII's	d	George, Duke of Gordon's

8 There's a statue of Queen Victoria at Queen's Cross. What's the name of the church the regal gaze looks out on?

a	Rubislaw	b	Carden Place
c	Beechgrove	d	St Ninian's

9 In the 1820s, the arches of the Mercat Cross at the Castlegate were boarded up and a door was constructed to allow it to function as what?

a	A ticket office for southbound coaches	b	The city's main post office
c	The city's main records office	d	The city's main dole office

10 The Mercat Cross has a sculpture of what on top of it?

a	A lion	b	A sheep
c	A unicorn	d	A knight in armour

11 A statue of which poet stands in the grounds of Aberdeen Grammar School?

a	John Keats	b	Percy Bysshe Shelley
c	Lord Byron	d	William McGonagall

12 Somewhere in the city, there are sculpted reliefs of a naked woman riding a stylised horse. Called *The Spirit of the Winds*, where can you see them?

a	Above the entrances to the housing block, Rosemount Square	b	On the entrance wall of the Trinity Shopping Centre
c	On the wall of the Central Library	d	On the fountain in Victoria Park

13 Where is Provost Ross's house?

a	Guestrow	b	Shiprow
c	Exchequer Row	d	Adelphi

14 And Provost Ross's house now forms part of which museum?

a	The Cloth-Making Museum	b	The Quarrying Museum
c	The Maritime Museum	d	The Paper-Making Museum

15 The city's cathedral in Old Aberdeen is named after which saint?

a	St Nicholas	b	St Machar
c	St Andrew	d	St Fittick

16 If you had arranged to meet somebody at the 'Monkey House', where would you expect to see them?

a	At the Commercial Union offices on the corner of Union Terrace	**b**	At Marks and Spencer's
c	At Hazlehead Zoo	**d**	In Archibald Simpson's

17 Which of the city's parks boasts a huge maze?

a	Westburn	**b**	Hazlehead
c	Duthie	**d**	Seaton

18 There's a stream that runs through the centre of the city, sometimes disappearing underground. What's its name?

a	Caveburn	**b**	Lairburn
c	Denburn	**d**	Cavernburn

19 A lighthouse overlooks Balnagask Golf Course. What's its name?

a	Girdleness	**b**	Beltness
c	Corsetness	**d**	Garterness

20 Who designed the lighthouse?

a	Robert Stevenson Sr	**b**	Thomas Smith
c	Davy Jones	**d**	Frederic S Morong Jr

21 Where is the city's Catholic cathedral?

a	Crown Street	b	Summer Street
c	Chapel Street	d	Huntly Street

22 And what's its name?

a	St Margaret's Cathedral	b	St Mary's Cathedral
c	St Mungo's Cathedral	d	St Matthew's Cathedral

23 Which of Aberdeen's housing estates is named after a Netherlands town?

a	Kincorth	b	Garthdee
c	Mastrick	d	Tillydrone

24 Approximately how long is Union Street?

a	Half a mile	b	A mile
c	Three-quarters of a mile	d	A mile and a quarter

25 What's the name of the hospital behind His Majesty's Theatre?

a	Woolmanhill	b	Fleecyknoll
c	Shagpile	d	Hairyheap

26 What would you find next to Robert Gordon's College?

a	Aberdeen Art Gallery	b	The Music Hall
c	The Central Library	d	Greyfriars Church

27 In Union Terrace, there's a statue of Burns holding something in his hand. Periodically stolen, what is it?

a	A book of his poems	b	A flower
c	A pen	d	A pair of women's knickers

28 Down at the seafront, there used to be a large red brick building. Demolished in the 1960s, what was its purpose?

a	A prison	b	Public swimming baths
c	A hospital	d	A school

29 The Bon-Accord Baths in Justice Mill Lane are also known as what?

a	The Uptoon Baths	b	The Doontoon Baths
c	The Central Baths	d	The Bonnie Baths

30 Erected around 1290, what's the name of the bridge over the Don in Old Aberdeen?

a	The Brig o' Sighs	b	The Brig o' Balgownie
c	The Brig o' Danestone	d	The Brig o' Seaton

31 In which of the city's park can you find a garden for blind and disabled people?

a	Westburn	b	Duthie
c	Victoria	d	Stewart

32 What's the name of the now disused theatre that stands on Guild Street, along from the bus and railway stations?

a	The Tivoli	b	The Globe
c	The Traverse	d	The Lyceum

33 What's the name of the extension to the Aberdeen Art Gallery?

a	Tufnell Hall	b	Cowdray Hall
c	Truman Hall	d	Sobers Hall

34 What used to stand on Great Northern Road between Ashgrove Road and the Northern Hotel?

a	A youth hostel	b	Kittybrewster Station
c	A dairy	d	A mart

35 What's the name of the long low hill down at The Links?

a	Ample Brae	b	Broad Hill
c	Wide Heights	d	Expansive Elevation

36 What's the dilapidated bridge across the Dee at Cults called?

a	Wobblin' Briggie	**b**	Shakkin' Briggie
c	Swayin' Briggie	**d**	Shudderin' Briggie

37 Whose statue stands on the rocks above the Leuchar Burn at Peterculter?

a	Rob Roy McGregor's	**b**	Ebbe Skovdhal's
c	Annie Lennox's	**d**	Robert the Bruce's

38 What was the name of the hotel in Cults that was destroyed in a tragic gas explosion?

a	The Marcliffe at Pitfodels	**b**	The Bieldside Inn
c	The Royal Darroch	**d**	The Royal Hotel

39 How many roads lead off the massive Mounthooly roundabout?

a	Four	**b**	Five
c	Six	**d**	Seven

40 You've decided to go to Rose Street for a kebab after a few drinks at The College. How do you get there?

a	You cross the road, head up Union Street and take the first left	**b**	You turn left and start walking – and walking and walking
c	You follow your nose	**d**	You turn right and go down Holburn Street

41 Where would you find Aberdeen's famous hostelry, Ma Cameron's (assuming you hadn't already been to The College)?

a	Little Belmont Street	b	Gaelic Lane
c	Back Wynd	d	Correction Wynd

42 A petition saved which of the city centre's bars from demolition? Clue – it has a famously long bar and serves some of the best stovies in town.

a	The Titled Wig	b	The Prince of Wales
c	Under The Hammer	d	The Blue Lumpie

43 What's the name of the small, port and fishing village near North Pier?

a	Handie	b	Fittie
c	Pinkie	d	Tummie

44 For many years, the city's main post office occupied an impressive granite building on which street?

a	Bon-Accord Street	b	Crown Street
c	Dee Street	d	Gordon Street

45 Where is the annual Offshore Europe shindig held?

a	The Beach Ballroom	b	Aberdeen Exhibition and Conference Centre
c	The Music Hall	d	Grunny Marshall's front room

46 Where are the Winter Gardens?

a	The Duthie Park	b	Hazlehead Park
c	Victoria Park	d	Seaton Park

47 We've met two of the city's cathedrals. What's the name of the third one?

a	St Andrew's	b	St Matthew's
c	St Luke's	d	St Mark's

48 And which famous US citizen visited this cathedral in his youth?

a	John F Kennedy	b	Bill Clinton
c	John Wayne	d	Elvis Presley

49 What's the defence site at Torry called?

a	The Torry Generator	b	The Torry Battery
c	The Torry Assault	d	The Torry Martello

50 With its streams, ponds and rustic bridges, what's the name of the small park on Viewfield Road?

a	Johnston Gardens	b	Anderson Gardens
c	Paterson Gardens	d	Davidson Gardens

2

History

Fa wiz fa an' fit wiz fit

Compared to other parts of Scotland, the history of the country's third city isn't very badly stained by the blood of battles or power struggles. Occasionally, there have been difficult times but these have been more than matched by examples of civic pride and joy. It has been argued that Aberdeen's greatest historical moment came on a rain-drenched night, in 1983, many miles away in a certain Swedish city – but more of that later.

1 What is the population of Aberdeen believed to have been around the year 1200?

a	9,000	b	6,000
c	3,000	d	1,200

2 When was Aberdeen granted a royal charter to give it burgh status?

a	1109	b	1179
c	1079	d	1209

3 Who granted the charter for this?

a	David I	b	William the Lion
c	William Wallace	d	Robert the Bruce

4 Who is the patron saint of Aberdeen?

a	St Nicholas	b	St Machar
c	St Andrew	d	St Mary

5 During the Middle Ages, Aberdeen did business with members of which trading alliance?

a	Hanseatic League	b	Footseatic League
c	Headseatic League	d	Bumseatic League

6 When was Old Aberdeen officially incorporated as part of the city?

a	1290	**b**	1490
c	1690	**d**	1890

7 What is the city's motto?

a	Bon Chance	**b**	Bon Voyage
c	Bon Accord	**d**	Bon Appétit

8 Union Street got its name in honour of what?

a	The Treaty of Union between Britain and Ireland	**b**	The Treaty of Union between England and Scotland
c	The marriage union between Queen Victoria and Prince Albert	**d**	The opening of the Edinburgh and Glasgow Union Canal

9 Which two creatures appear on Aberdeen's coat of arms?

a	A ram and a ewe	**b**	Two leopards
c	A lion and a unicorn	**d**	An elephant and a mouse

10 There are three towers on the coat of arms. What do they represent?

a	The church, the state and education	**b**	Trust, thrift and tolerance
c	The three times AFC have beaten the Old Firm in recent memory	**d**	The three hills the city is built on

11 Which street was originally intended to be the city's main street?

a	King Street	b	Broad Street
c	George Street	d	Market Street

12 In which year was the Trinity Centre opened?

a	1975	b	1995
c	1965	d	1985

13 When was the International Youth Festival first held?

a	1983	b	1973
c	1963	d	1953

14 When was the Music Hall opened?

a	1832	b	1822
c	1842	d	1812

15 What, according to the first census of 1801, was the population of the city?

a	27,000	b	17,000
c	37,000	d	7,000

16 When did Aberdeen get its first railway connection?

a	1830	b	1850
c	1840	d	1860

17 And when did the first steam trawlers appear?

a	1842	b	1862
c	1882	d	1902

18 In which year was St Nicholas House built?

a	1967	b	1947
c	1957	d	1977

19 Who granted the city charters in recognition of Aberdonians' help against the English in the Scottish Wars of Independence?

a	William Wallace	b	Robert the Bruce
c	Bonnie Prince Charlie	d	Duke of Argyll

20 He also bestowed one of his royal hunting forests on the city. What was its name?

a	Stocket	b	Drumoak
c	Countesswells	d	Funky

21 The forest subsequently became known as what?

a	Liberty Lands	b	Independence Lands
c	Autonomy Lands	d	Freedom Lands

22 Sixty-seven stones mark the inner boundaries of these lands. What are they called?

a	Tramp Stones	b	March Stones
c	Tread Stones	d	Pace Stones

23 As well as the royal hunting forest, funds were also donated for the building of what?

a	A new branch of the Copie	b	The Brig o' Balgownie
c	King's College	d	The Mercat Cross

24 Which English king destroyed huge parts of Aberdeen in 1337 in retaliation for this help?

a	Edward I	b	Edward II
c	Edward III	d	Edward IV

25 What's the name of the much-moved wellhead, first erected in 1708, that now stands at the Castlegate?

a	The Mannie Well	b	The Wifie Well
c	The Lounie Well	d	The Quinie Well

26 By 1861, the census showed the population had risen to . . .?

a	34,000	b	54,000
c	94,000	d	74,000

27 Which town is thought to be the oldest on Deeside?

a	Banchory	b	Ballater
c	Aboyne	d	Kincardine O'Neil

28 Where in the city was a leprosy hospital founded in 1363?

a	Spital Hill	b	Broad Hill
c	Summer Hill	d	Stocket Hill

29 When was the last recorded case of leprosy in the city?

a	1500s	b	1600s
c	1700s	d	1800s

30 In which year was Aberdeen struck by a typhoid epidemic?

a	1962	b	1963
c	1964	d	1965

31 Who was the Chief Medical Officer of Health at the time?

a	Dr Andrew Prince	**b**	Dr Douglas King
c	Dr Morag Duke	**d**	Dr Ian MacQueen

32 The city was quarantined for how long?

a	Nearly a fortnight	**b**	Nearly a month
c	Nearly two months	**d**	Nearly six months

33 What was identified as the source of the outbreak?

a	Dodgy pies from Pittodrie	**b**	Corned beef from Argentina
c	Frogs' legs from France	**d**	Lamb from New Zealand

34 What's the name of the battle Robert the Bruce fought near Inverurie against Red Comyn in 1308?

a	Battle of Toon	**b**	Battle of City
c	Battle of Burg	**d**	Battle of Burra

35 One of Scotland's bloodiest battles was also fought near Inverurie – this time in 1411. Can you name it?

a	Battle of Harlaw	**b**	Battle of Northfield
c	Battle of Linksfield	**d**	Battle of St Machar

36 Legend has it that whose leg is immured in St Machar's Cathedral?

a	William Wallace's	b	Robert the Bruce's
c	Bonnie Prince Charlie's	d	John Balliol's

37 What went on at the traditional feein' markets?

a	Livestock was bought and sold	b	Property auctions were held
c	Agricultural workers were hired	d	Property rents were set

38 When were the biannual feein' markets held?

a	Christmas and Halloween	b	Whitsun and Martinmas
c	Easter and Lammas	d	Candlemas and New Year's Day

39 How many folk were living in the city by the time of the 1911 census?

a	164,000	b	104,000
c	124,000	d	144,000

40 What, originally, was a bothy?

a	A pig sty	b	A barn
c	A dog kennel	d	A hut where unmarried male farm workers lived

41 In 1664, which royalist plundered the city?

a	Duke of Dundee	b	Marquis of Montrose
c	Earl of Elgin	d	Prince of Peterhead

42 The perpetrator of this raid was later executed. Which part of his body was sent to the city as proof of his death?

a	His arm	b	His head
c	His heart	d	His leg

43 In the nineteenth century, Aberdeen's shipyards were world famous for the clippers they built to transport what?

a	Butteries	b	Tea
c	Cotton	d	Tobacco

44 When were electric trams introduced in the city?

a	1894	b	1904
c	1914	d	1924

45 When did the Cairngorm funicular railway first start running?

a	1971	b	1981
c	1991	d	2001

46 How did the Grampian Mountains get their name?

a	From the Gaelic for a high place	**b**	From the Latin name of a Roman battle site
c	From the Lowland Scots for a wild place	**d**	From the Doric meaning a bad-tempered place

47 What's the name of Aberdeen's Museum of Civic History?

a	Tolbooth Museum	**b**	Torry Museum
c	Castlegate Museum	**d**	People's Museum

48 What was the Wardhouse that forms part of this museum?

a	A hospital	**b**	A council chamber
c	A jail	**d**	A courtroom

49 In the museum you can see something called a 'maiden'. What was it used for?

a	Executions – it's a guillotine	**b**	Knocking down walls – it's a battering ram
c	Transport – it's a type of sedan chair	**d**	Farming – it's a type of plough blade

50 Currently, what's the population of the city?

a	About 215,000	**b**	About 150,000
c	About 500,000	**d**	About 275,000

3

Language
Div ye spik 'i Doric?

'Dinna say "dinna"!'

Advice from an Aberdeen schoolteacher to her class!

With its vowels bearing little or no resemblance to any of those of standard Scots, let alone standard English, understanding the Doric isn't easy. Add to that its peculiar vocabulary and some might say that, for those not blessed with having their roots in or around Aberdeen, it's impossible!

1 What's a 'quine' or 'quinie'?

a	A female cat	b	A girl
c	A ewe	d	A cow

2 And what's a 'loun' or 'lounie'?

a	A boy	b	A fool
c	A ram	d	A bull

3 What's a 'feel gype'?

a	A dirty look	b	A full stomach
c	A healthy bank balance	d	A really stupid person

4 If you were 'bleezin'', what state would you be in?

a	Very angry	b	Very sad
c	Very drunk	d	Very hungry

5 If you 'cowp' something, what do you do to it?

a	Swallow it	b	Knock it over
c	Thump it	d	Lose it

6 If someone's 'awa' fur a daunder', where are they?

a	Out for lunch	b	On a fag break
c	Taking a stroll	d	In the lavvy

7 If someone said 'Hiv ye hid yer eenfu'?', what would they asking you?

a	To stop staring	b	Whether you'd had too much to drink
c	Whether you'd had enough sleep	d	Whether you'd had your supper

8 If you say you have a 'youkie doup', what have you got?

a	An eggy face	b	An itchy bum
c	A comfy chair	d	An upset stomach

9 When would you call on the services of a 'howdie'?

a	When a baby's about to be born – she's a midwife	b	When you've got blocked drains – he's a plumber
c	When you're redecorating – he's a painter	d	When your dog's not well – she's a vet

10 What do you get if you get a 'fleg'?

a	A flea bite	b	A shock
c	An unexpected present	d	A cold

11 What should you avoid doing with a person who's known as a 'claik'?

a	Going to Pittodrie – a 'claik' is a Celtic supporter	**b**	Telling them a secret – a 'claik' is a gossip
c	Going to a pub quiz – a 'claik' is a stupid person	**d**	Making a mess – a 'claik' is a pernickety person

12 If someone asked 'Far d'ye bide?', what would they want to know?

a	What your name is	**b**	What you do for a living
c	Where you stay	**d**	How old you are

13 If you asked someone for a 'bosie', what would you want?

a	A loan of money	**b**	A cuddle
c	A lift	**d**	A racing tip

14 If someone said to you 'Dinna fash yersel'.', what would they be advising you to do?

a	Not to have any more to drink	**b**	Not to wear such unfashionable clothes
c	Not to pick your nose in public	**d**	Not to worry

15 Where would you wear your 'beets'?

a	On your feet – they're boots	**b**	On your hands – they're mitts
c	On your bottom – they're knickers	**d**	On your head – they're earmuffs

16 Somebody greets you with 'Fit like 'i day, min?'. What are they saying?

a	Where have you been?	b	How are you today, sir?
c	Have you recovered from last night's drinking session?	d	Have you got a light?

17 Someone asks how you are and you reply 'Ah'm jist tyauvin' (pronounced chavvin) awa''. What does this mean?

a	I'm struggling on	b	I'm feeling fine
c	I'm a bit knackered	d	I'm far too hot

18 If someone's face is described as being like 'a skelpit erse', what does it resemble?

a	A burst paper bag	b	A smacked bottom
c	A beetroot	d	The back end of a bus

19 If your mum shouts at you for 'pitting dubs on 'i clean fleer', what have you done?

a	Spilt beans on the floor	b	Dropped crumbs on the floor
c	Made the floor all muddy	d	Dripped Irn-Bru on the floor

20 If you're 'speirin'', what are you doing?

a	Stabbing someone	b	Asking someone questions
c	Criticising someone	d	Loving someone

21 If you answered the door in your 'semmit', what would you be wearing?

a	A towelling bathrobe	**b**	A sexy negligee
c	A vest	**d**	Nothing

22 Which of the following best describes a bairn that is 'thrawn'?

a	Well behaved and docile	**b**	Quiet and loving
c	Cheeky and lively	**d**	Naughty and difficult to control

23 Which of these means empty?

a	Teem	**b**	Stappit
c	Raivelt	**d**	Sossy

24 What's a 'tourie'?

a	A tourist	**b**	A woolly hat with a pom-pom
c	A holiday	**d**	A visit to the toilet

25 If a cat's 'raxin' oot', what's it doing?

a	Spending the night on the tiles	**b**	Having a good stretch
c	Stalking prey	**d**	Yowling loudly

26 Who would wear 'dungars'?

a	A workman – they're overalls	**b**	A surgeon – they're thin rubber gloves
c	A jockey – they're racing colours	**d**	A cook – they're chef's whites

27 If someone asked you for a 'spunk', what would they be wanting?

a	A safety pin for their burst breeks	**b**	A boost to get them over a wall, etc.
c	A word of encouragement	**d**	A match or a light for their fag

28 What are you doing to the tatties if you're 'breein'' them?

a	Peeling them	**b**	Mashing them
c	Draining them	**d**	Buttering them

29 If somebody asked you to do something 'ivnoo', when would they expect you to do it?

a	Straightaway	**b**	After you've had a cup of tea
c	When you get the chance	**d**	Tomorrow

30 If a person 'hirples', what do they do?

a	Walk with a limp	**b**	Talk with a lisp
c	Shake nervously	**d**	Fiddle about

31 What are 'chuckies'?

a	Chickens	b	Granite chips
c	Children	d	Jokes

32 If something's 'foostie', what's wrong with it?

a	It's old-fashioned	b	It doesn't work properly
c	It's rotten	d	It's lost

33 If you heard somebody say 'Gyaaaaaaaads!', what would they be expressing?

a	Delight	b	Disgust
c	Dissatisfaction	d	Anger

34 If someone asked you 'Fit's adee?', what would they mean?

a	What's the matter?	b	What's this for?
c	What's the time?	d	What's your name?

35 If somebody's 'a bittie dottilt', what are they?

a	Slightly tipsy	b	A little confused
c	Rather mean	d	Somewhat deaf

36 What's a 'bachle'?

a	An old worn-out shoe	**b**	A back garden
c	A ride on the back of somebody's bike	**d**	A baked tattie

37 If you were wearing 'gey nippit brikks', what would you have on?

a	Shorts that are somewhat revealing	**b**	Shoes with laces that are rather short
c	Jeans that are a bit old and worn looking	**d**	Trousers that are on the tight side

38 If you told somebody 'Ah'm gan tae a pluntin' 'i day', what would you mean?

a	I'm off to play golf today	**b**	I'm attending a funeral today
c	I'm up in court today	**d**	I've got the dentist today

39 Who would wear a 'hippen'?

a	A worker on a building site, etc. – it's a hard hat	**b**	A baby – it's a nappy
c	A joiner – it's a tool belt	**d**	A grunny – it's a shawl

40 If someone is 'foggin'', what are they?

a	Poor	**b**	Disorientated
c	Wealthy	**d**	Smelly

41 If somebody said you were 'grippy', would you be pleased?

a	No – it means dirty	b	Yes – it means clever
c	No – it means mean	d	Yes – it means good-looking

42 If someone gave you a 'kittle', what would you do?

a	Say thanks – it's a fiver	b	Feel upset – it's an insult
c	Laugh – it's a tickle	d	Run away – it's a threat

43 What's a 'cuttie'?

a	A knife	b	A slice of ham
c	A short tobacco pipe	d	A sausage

44 What do you do to somebody if you 'clype' on them?

a	Tell tales about them	b	Spill beer on them
c	Bump into them	d	Have a row with them

45 What does a 'scaffie' do for a living?

a	Builds scaffolding	b	Teaches domestic science
c	Guts and cleans fish	d	Sweeps the streets

46 What's a 'redd-up'?

a	A session of cleaning and tidying	b	A game of snooker
c	A pub crawl	d	A convincing win for the Dons

47 If you bend back your finger and hurt it, what have you done to it?

a	Cleft it	b	Scored it
c	Noted it	d	Staived it

48 If you were caught 'chorin'', what would you have been doing?

a	Driving without insurance	b	Peeing in the street
c	Stealing	d	Dodging your Council Tax

49 Where would a 'chunty' be kept?

a	Under the bed – it's a chamber pot	b	In the kitchen cupboard – it's a jar of pickles
c	In the garden shed – it's a type of spade	d	Outside – it's a large dustbin

50 How would you describe a room that's dusty?

a	Poorie	b	Stoorie
c	Boorie	d	Choorie

4

Work
Fit div ye dee?

'Work is the curse of the
drinking classes.'

Oscar Wilde

Aberdeen somehow brings out the inventive side of its folk – if one way of earning
a living goes into decline, another one soon takes its place. When fish and granite
became less lucrative, along came the North Sea oil industry. And now, as more
eco-friendly ways of energy production are required, the skills learned in oil and
gas production will, no doubt, be tapped to ensure the city is at the forefront of
developing the technology for wind and wave power.

1 Established in Aberdeen in 1136, what is Britain's oldest business?

a	Milne's Wig-making	**b**	Berryden Dairies
c	The Inversnecky Cafe	**d**	Aberdeen Harbour Board

2 It was founded in Aberdeen in 1498 and is still in business today. Can you name the world's oldest transport company?

a	Clarke and Rose	**b**	The Shore Porters Society
c	Copie Flitters	**d**	Pickfords

3 *The Aberdeen Journal*, a forerunner of the *Press and Journal*, is one of Britain's oldest newspapers. When was it first printed?

a	1748	**b**	1598
c	1328	**d**	1668

4 Robert Davidson of Aberdeen worked in the early nineteenth century developing something we all take for granted today. What?

a	Toothpaste	**b**	The postal service
c	Electric motors	**d**	Rowies

5 What were the surnames of the owners of the textile mill at Granholm?

a	Crombie and Knowles	**b**	Burberry and Knowles
c	Oormannie and Knowles	**d**	Gucci and Knowles

6 What kind of business was Isaac Benzies?

a	A furniture store	b	An undertaker's
c	A department store	d	A tea room

7 What was the name of the sporting goods store that formerly stood on George Street?

a	The Rubber Shop	b	The Latex Shop
c	The Resin shop	d	The Gum Shop

8 From 1903 to 1972, what did Cocky Hunter's sell?

a	Real ale and stovies	b	Any kind of game you cared to ask for
c	Tiger skins	d	Bric-a-brac and second-hand stuff

9 And what is Cocky Hunter's nowadays?

a	An aviary in the Duthie Park	b	A city centre pub
c	A fast food outlet at the beach	d	Any untidy place

10 A long-time favourite with Aberdonians, what's the name of the restaurant just past Union Bridge?

a	Victoria	b	Albert
c	Posh	d	Becks

11 The restaurant is above which of the city's jeweller's shops?

a	Finnies	b	John Park
c	Ernest Jones	d	Jamieson and Carry

12 What are silver darlings?

a	Particularly sparkly bits of granite	b	Herring
c	A swanky seafood restaurant	d	Polite older shop assistants

13 What were Fifies and Zulus?

a	Types of dressed granite	b	Types of herring fishing boats
c	Types of textile looms	d	Large paper sizes

14 Which of these is a common way of fishing for herring?

a	Coast netting	b	Wander netting
c	Drift netting	d	Stray netting

15 Fishermen believe that catching which fish at sea is unlucky?

a	Pike	b	Salmon
c	Goldfish	d	Minnow

16 On which day of the week did whalers never set sail because it was thought to be unlucky?

a	Friday	b	Saturday
c	Sunday	d	Monday

17 And which kind of a person is thought to bring bad luck to fishing boats?

a	A doctor	b	A lawyer
c	A clergyman	d	A teacher

18 Some trawlers use long vertically hanging nets called . . .?

a	Rhine nets	b	Danube nets
c	Seine nets	d	Thames nets

19 What, in arable farming, was the 'guidman's grund'?

a	A herb garden	b	An area left unplanted to appease the devil
c	An area where soft fruits were grown	d	A compost heap

20 Which rock is most commonly seen on the Earth's surface?

a	Sandstone	b	Limestone
c	Edinburgh	d	Granite

21 What type of rock is granite?

a	Igneous	b	Affyhard
c	Metamorphic	d	Sedimentary

22 What's the name for the glittery bitties in granite?

a	Sequins	b	Mica
c	Tinsel	d	Crystals

23 640,000 cubic feet of Aberdeen granite went into building of what?

a	St Nicholas House	b	The Kremlin, Moscow
c	The Forth Rail Bridge	d	The Sidney Opera House

24 Where is John Fyffe's Paradise Quarry?

a	Parkheid	b	Kemnay
c	Banchory	d	Inverurie

25 In which decade did Rubislaw Quarry close?

a	1970s	b	1950s
c	1930s	d	1990s

26 From which north-east town does the delicious Rizza's ice cream hail?

a	Turriff	b	Methlick
c	Mintlaw	d	Huntly

27 Officially, when did North Sea oil first come ashore?

a	1970	b	1978
c	1972	d	1975

28 From which oilfield did it flow?

a	Forties	b	Brent
c	Thistle	d	Beryl

29 Who inaugurated its flow?

a	Harold Wilson	b	The Queen
c	Prince Charles	d	Sir Ian Wood

30 And where did the oil come ashore?

a	Sullom Voe	b	St Fergus
c	Cruden Bay	d	Flotta

31 What is the name of famous oil industry firefighter?

a	'Red' Comyn	b	'Black' Dog
c	'Red' Adair	d	'Black' Douglas

32 In 2002, the biggest discovery of North Sea oil in over a decade was made. In which field?

a	Buzzard	b	Kestrel
c	Budgie	d	Falcon

33 What's the name of the Roger Moore character in the oil rig thriller movie *North Sea Hijack?*

a	fforbes	b	Llewelyn
c	ffolkes	d	Lloyd

34 What has been businessman Bob Farquhar's contribution to the North Sea oil industry?

a	Offshore catering	b	Supply of portable toilets
c	Supply of protective clothing	d	Supply of drawing office equipment

35 What's a labourer on an oilrig called?

a	A roustabout	b	A turnabout
c	A rouseabout	d	A roundabout

36 First produced in an Aberdeen textile mill, what is a Crombie?

a	A cashmere overcoat	b	A beige checked baseball cap
c	A knitted scarf	d	A woolly vest

37 What's the name of the north-east village where the food-producer Baxter's is based?

a	Foggieloan	b	Fettercairn
c	Fordoun	d	Fochabers

38 What was the name of the Hatton-based biscuit producers?

a	Simmers	b	Winters
c	Springs	d	Tunnocks

39 When was Aberdeen's first shipyard founded?

a	1653	b	1853
c	1753	d	1553

40 Which was the last Aberdeen shipyard to close?

a	Hall Russell	b	John Brown
c	Harland and Wolff	d	Yarrows

41 Which three ingredients are needed to make whisky?

a	Water, yeast and barley	b	Water, hops and wheat
c	Water, yeast and wheat	d	Water, hops and rice

42 What is the name of the sugary liquid produced at the start of the whisky-making process?

a	Mash	b	Wort
c	Plook	d	Malt

43 In which Banffshire town is Glenfiddich whisky produced?

a	Knockando	b	Portsoy
c	Gardenstown	d	Dufftown

44 Where, in the north-east, is Walker's shortbread produced?

a	Aberlour	b	Alford
c	Kintore	d	Kemnay

45 What's the name of the paper mill at Stoneywood?

a	Arjo Toupees	b	Arjo Wiggins
c	Arjo Extensions	d	Arjo Hairpieces

46 What was Lawsons of Dyce famous for producing?

a	Sofas	b	Sports equipment
c	Sausages	d	String

47 Which famous architect designed the Aberdeen Business School at Garthdee?

a	Sir Norman Foster	b	Robert Adam
c	Sir Christopher Wren	d	Sir Edwin Lutyens

48 Where is Thainstone Mart, the most modern livestock market in Europe?

a	Oldmeldrum	b	Fyvie
c	Kintore	d	Stonehaven

49 Which Aberdeenshire company is famous for its milk and ice-cream production?

a	Mackies	b	Michies
c	Mitchells	d	Massies

50 Aberdeen's is the busiest in the world. Aberdeen's what?

a	Branch of Marks and Spencer	b	Heliport
c	Citizens' Advice Bureau	d	Livestock market

5
Culture
Fit's 'at??

'Your search for "culture" in Aberdeen, United Kingdom returned 0 results.'

Internet search message!

Huh! What do they know? Nihin' is the answer! Aberdeen has always had a diverse and vibrant cultural scene – as the following fifty questions prove.

1 Aberdeen has won the Britain in Bloom a record number of times. How many?

a	Ten	b	Twelve
c	Seven	d	Eight

2 September 1896 saw a significant first for Aberdeen's Music Hall. What was it?

a	It was the venue of Harry Lauder's first professional appearance	b	It screened 18 short films over three days and was, therefore, the city's first cinema
c	It was the venue of Houdini's first British stage show	d	Buffalo Bill's first British Wild West show was staged there

3 What type of classical columns can be seen at the front of the Music Hall?

a	Ionic	b	Doric
c	Composite	d	Corinthian

4 Where, traditionally, is the amateur Christmas pantomime held?

a	The Music Hall	b	St Nichols Church Graveyard
c	His Majesty's Theatre	d	Aberdeen Arts Centre

5 And which theatre group puts on the panto?

a	The Loft Theatre Group	b	The Attic Theatre Group
c	The Behind-the-Scenes Theatre Group	d	The Bedroom Farce Theatre Group

6 Is this amateur panto generally considered to be better than its professional rival at HMT?

a	Oh, yes, it is	**b**	Oh, no, it isn't
c	Aye, iv coorse it is	**d**	Nae chunce

7 What's the name of the annual market held at the Castlegate?

a	Scunner Market	**b**	Timmer Market
c	Simmer Market	**d**	Feein' Market

8 And what was the original purpose of this market?

a	The sale of textiles	**b**	The sale of sweeties
c	The sale of wooden goods	**d**	The hiring of labourers

9 How many official twin towns does Aberdeen have?

a	Five	**b**	Six
c	Four	**d**	Seven

10 What's the name of the festival held in July and August each year?

a	Aberdeen International Young Musicians' Festival	**b**	Aberdeen International All Singing and Dancing Festival
c	Aberdeen International Fish Festival	**d**	Aberdeen International Youth Festival

11 What's the name of the venue on West North Street?

a	The Apple Tree	b	The Fig Tree
c	The Cherry Tree	d	The Lemon Tree

12 His Majesty's Theatre is about to be twinned with another HMT. Where is it?

a	Perth, Australia	b	Toronto, Canada
c	Wellington, New Zealand	d	Boston, USA

13 Which north-east town is known as 'The Bloo Toon'?

a	Stonehaven	b	Peterhead
c	Banchory	d	Ballater

14 What was the Tivoli Theatre formerly known as?

a	His Majesty's Music Hall	b	His Majesty's Playhouse
c	His Majesty's Opera House	d	His Majesty's Concert Hall

15 What's the name of the National Trust gardens near Ellon?

a	Balmedie	b	Pitmedden
c	Methlick	d	Fyvie

16 The year 2003 saw Aberdeen FC celebrate its centenary. What sporting event also reached its one-hundredth anniversary in that year?

a	The Wimbledon Championships	**b**	The Embassy World Snooker Championship
c	The Tour de France	**d**	The University Boat Race

17 Forvie Nature Reserve is close to which town?

a	Newburgh	**b**	Collieston
c	Cruden Bay	**d**	Stonehaven

18 Which hill would you climb to reach the peak known as Mither Tap?

a	Lochnagar	**b**	Ben Macdhui
c	Cairn o'Mounth	**d**	Bennachie

19 Which Aberdeenshire town holds a Doric festival in October each year?

a	Inverurie	**b**	Ellon
c	Udny	**d**	Alford

20 Which French town is Aberdeen twinned with?

a	Lyons	**b**	Rheims
c	Clermont-Ferrand	**d**	Marseilles

21 Slains Castle is thought to be the site that inspired the creation of which literary character?

| a | Frankenstein's monster | b | Count Dracula |
| c | Freddy Krueger | d | The Boogeyman |

22 Which north-east castle was used as the backdrop for Zeffirelli's film version of *Hamlet*?

| a | Craigievar Castle | b | Drum Castle |
| c | Castle Fraser | d | Dunnotter Castle |

23 Attended by the royal family, what is the name best-known Highland Games?

| a | The Braemar Gathering | b | The Garioch Get-Thegither |
| c | The Alford Assembly | d | The Muchalls Meeting |

24 The modern games were first held in 1832 but who is said to have inaugurated them many years before that?

| a | Queen Victoria | b | Billy Connolly |
| c | Malcolm Ceann-mor | d | William Wallace |

25 Where in the north east is there a transport museum?

| a | Ballater | b | Alford |
| c | Huntly | d | Peterhead |

26 What's the name of the comedy team, popular in the 1970s and 1980s, whose sketches and songs were in Doric?

a	Scotland the What?	**b**	Grumpian the Fa?
c	Aiberdeen the Fit?	**d**	Peterheid the Fit Wey?

27 Which of the following was not a member of this comedy team?

a	Buff Hardie	**b**	Douglas Kynoch
c	Stephen Robertson	**d**	George Donald

28 What, according to the Scotland the What? team, is a 'futret'?

a	A low Japanese bed	**b**	A gorse bush
c	A footstool	**d**	A ferret

29 And they suggest which of the following is how 'futret' should be spelt?

a	FUTRIT	**b**	FUTRET
c	FITRIT	**d**	FERRET

30 Which German town is Aberdeen twinned with?

a	Mannheim	**b**	Leipzig
c	Regensburg	**d**	Stuttgart

31 Which north-east personality presents Radio Scotland's weekly country dance music show?

a	Bobby Farmer	b	Sandy Swain
c	Robbie Shepherd	d	Sarah Cox

32 There used to be a small zoo in the city. Where was it?

a	Duthie Park	b	Hazlehead Park
c	Seaton Park	d	Union Terrace Gardens

33 What do people flock to the Falls of Feuch at Banchory to see?

a	White-water rafting	b	Ospreys nesting
c	Salmon leaping upstream	d	A species of orchid that grows nowhere else

34 Where in Aberdeen is the Gordon Highlanders Museum?

a	Just off Queen's Road	b	Bridge of Don
c	Footdee	d	Crown Street

35 What can unexpectedly be found in the Mannofield area of the city?

a	Five streets of red-brick houses dating from the nineteenth century	b	A cricket ground
c	A house occupied by a poor lawyer	d	The only remaining air raid shelter in the city

36 What exciting activity can you take part in at Kaimhill?

a	Queuing to get in to Asda	**b**	Skiing on the dry ski slope
c	Attending a weekly farmers' market	**d**	Line-dancing classes in B&Q's car park

37 Which of the actors in *The Bill* was born in Aberdeen?

a	Daniel MacPherson	**b**	Paul Usher
c	Alex Walkinshaw	**d**	Jeff Stewart

38 And which character does he play?

a	Reg Hollis	**b**	Cameron Tait
c	Des Taviner	**d**	Dale Smith

39 While Robbie Shepherd was on holiday in 2003, who presented his *The Reel Blend* Scottish country dance music radio programme?

a	Darius Danesh	**b**	Cameron Stout
c	Will Young	**d**	David Sneddon

40 Which Norwegian town is Aberdeen twinned with?

a	Stavanger	**b**	Bergen
c	Trondheim	**d**	Tromsø

41 Who's the Aberdonian who presents the Radio 3 arts programme *Night Waves*?

a	Annie Cummings	**b**	Cathy Holburn
c	Jane Seaton	**d**	Isabel Hilton

42 Which north-east town has an annual Hogmanay Fireball Festival?

a	Stonehaven	**b**	Inverurie
c	Banchory	**d**	Ellon

43 Which town in Belarus is Aberdeen twinned with?

a	Gomel	**b**	Minsk
c	Babruysk	**d**	Salihorsk

44 When did Grampian TV first appear on our tellies?

a	1958	**b**	1961
c	1959	**d**	1960

45 Which north-east town is known as 'The Broch'?

a	Peterhead	**b**	Huntly
c	Fraserburgh	**d**	Inverurie

46 What's the name of the walk that runs from Bennachie to Rhynie?

a	The West Gordon Way	**b**	The Garioch Trail
c	The Thainstone Trachle	**d**	The Pitcaple Path

47 Just north of Pitmedden, there's a house that was built by the second Earl of Aberdeen in 1731. What's its name?

a	Haddo House	**b**	Monboddo House
c	Leith Hall	**d**	Aden House

48 Haddo House is famous for what?

a	Its ballet company	**b**	Its theatre company
c	Its puppet shows	**d**	Its opera company

49 Which town in Zimbabwe is Aberdeen twinned with?

a	Harare	**b**	Bulawayo
c	Mutare	**d**	Gweru

50 Where is the north-east's Agricultural Heritage Centre?

a	Aden Country Park	**b**	Balmedie Beach and Country Park
c	Millbuies Country Park	**d**	Monkie Country Park

6
Football
Fan's 'i fitba' on?

'Some people think football is a matter of life and death. I don't like that attitude. I can assure them it is much more serious than that.'

Bill Shankley

Football means an awful lot to many Aberdonians. At the time of writing, our league position isn't great and even the most loyal fans will concede that things are at bit of a low ebb(e). Having tasted success at the highest level, the current poor showing is all the harder to take. But the Pittodrie faithful still dream of singing 'A European Song' again and of recapturing the glory days that culminated in Gothenburg. Well, maybe not both – the football was fab but, you have to admit it, that song was rubbish! Kids growing up in the 1980s knew nothing else but basking in the reflected glory that following the winning ways of a top team offers. Let's hope a return to the big time is just around the corner.

So, here we go, as they say. We'll kick-off with not just Aberdeen's best but possibly Scotland's best ever player.

C'MON EWE REDZ

1 He never played for the Dons but Denis Law is undoubtedly Aberdeen's most famous footballing son. At which club did he spend most of his career?

a	Manchester City	**b**	Chelsea
c	Manchester United	**d**	Leeds United

2 Which boys' club did Denis play for?

a	Aberdeen Lads' Club	**b**	Banks o' Dee
c	Rosemount	**d**	Sunnybank

3 And which English club first signed the young Lawman?

a	Stockport County	**b**	Huddersfield Town
c	Wigan Athletic	**d**	Rochdale

4 Law became the first £100,000 footballer when he signed for which Italian club?

a	Torino	**b**	Inter Milan
c	Lazio	**d**	Juventus

5 How many caps did Denis Law win for Scotland?

a	82	**b**	39
c	102	**d**	55

6 And how many international goals did Law score to make him Scotland's joint top scorer?

a	30	b	19
c	42	d	25

7 Denis Law shares this record with . . .?

a	Archie Gemmill	b	Joe Jordan
c	Colin Stein	d	Kenny Dalglish

8 Which club was the last one to have Denis on its books?

a	Manchester City	b	Chelsea
c	Manchester United	d	Leeds United

9 And, in the twilight of his playing career, which team's relegation was sealed by a Denis Law goal?

a	Crystal Palace	b	Wolverhampton Wanderers
c	Manchester United	d	Everton

10 Now for Aberdeen's greatest achievement – winning the European Cup-Winners' Cup in 1983. Which mighty team did the Dons beat in the final?

a	Real Madrid	b	Ajax Amsterdam
c	Inter Milan	d	Bayern Munich

11 In which Scandinavian city was the final played?

a	Copenhagen	b	Oslo
c	Gothenburg	d	Stockholm

12 Can you name the stadium that staged the rain-drenched final?

a	Nya Ullevi	b	Uvgotmi
c	Globen	d	Råsunda

13 Who was the manager this cup-winning side?

a	Alex Ferguson	b	Billy McNeill
c	Jimmy Bonthrone	d	Ally McLeod

14 And who captained the team?

a	Alex McLeish	b	Willie Miller
c	Jim Leighton	d	Gordon Strachan

15 Who scored Aberdeen's winning goal?

a	Mark McGhee	b	John Hewitt
c	Eric Black	d	Gordon Strachan

16 The final score was 2–1. Who scored Aberdeen's other goal?

a	Mark McGhee	b	Peter Weir
c	Eric Black	d	Gordon Strachan

17 And who scored the opposition's goal?

a	Isidro San José Pozo	b	José Antonio Camacho
c	Carlos Alonso González ('Santillana')	d	Juan Gómez González ('Juanito')

18 Which team did the Dandies beat to secure their place in the final?

a	Waterschei	b	Feyenoord
c	Anderlecht	d	Borussia Moenchengladbach

19 Some more recent European escapades. Which team knocked Aberdeen out of Europe in the season 2002–03?

a	Hamburg	b	Paris St Germain
c	Hertha Berlin	d	Boavista

20 Which of the Dandies' players was sent off in the away leg against this team?

a	Eric Deloumeaux	b	Roberto Bisconti
c	Derek Whyte	d	Peter Kjaer

21 In the previous season, Aberdeen suffered a humiliating defeat in Europe against which team of part-timers?

a	Bohemians (Eire)	**b**	Nistru Otaci (Moldova)
c	Cwmbran (Wales)	**d**	Trondheim (Norway)

22 Some historical stuff. The name Pittodrie comes from Gaelic and means what?

a	Gallows Hill	**b**	Hill of Dung
c	Ant Hill	**d**	Broad Hill

23 The club was founded in 1903. According to the records, what was the exact date?

a	09 June	**b**	14 April
c	27 May	**d**	04 July

24 What was the name of the club's first manager?

a	Jimmy Philip	**b**	Philip James
c	Tommy Pearson	**d**	Peter Thomson

25 In which season did the team first wear red tops?

a	1945–46	**b**	1921–22
c	1913–14	**d**	1938–39

26 What colour of jerseys did the Dons wear prior to that?

a	Black and white vertical stripes	**b**	Yellow and black vertical stripes
c	Yellow and black hoops	**d**	Black and white hoops

27 The colours of their jerseys gave rise to what early nickname for the team?

a	The Bees	**b**	The Zebras
c	The Wasps	**d**	The Tabbies

28 And in which year did they adopt the current all-red strip?

a	1966	**b**	1946
c	1976	**d**	1956

29 In the Scottish Cup in 1923, the Dons notched up a record number of goals scored in a single game. How many did they score?

a	9	**b**	11
c	13	**d**	15

30 And which club was on the receiving end of this torrent of goals?

a	Fraserburgh	**b**	Arbroath
c	Montrose	**d**	Peterhead

31 Until season 2003–04, he was still doing the job he'd held for many, many years. What is the name of this long-serving kit man?

a	Eddie English	b	Teddy Scott
c	Ted Wales	d	Ed Ireland

32 Aberdeen's domestic record. In which season did Aberdeen first win the First Division title?

a	1933–34	b	1942–43
c	1948–49	d	1954–55

33 And how many times in total did the Pittodrie side win this title?

a	Six times	b	Eight times
c	Three times	d	Once

34 How many times have the Dons won the Scottish Premier League Championship?

a	Once	b	Twice
c	Three times	d	Four times

35 How many times has the team won the Scottish Cup?

a	Six times	b	Seven times
c	Eight times	d	Nine times

36 And for how many consecutive seasons was this trophy Pittodrie bound?

a	Two	b	Three
c	Four	d	Five

37 How many times has an Aberdeen captain picked up the League Cup?

a	Four times	b	Five times
c	Six times	d	Seven times

38 Which team did Aberdeen beat to win the European Super Cup?

a	Bayern Munich	b	FC Utrecht
c	Borussia Dortmund	d	Hamburg

39 The record crowd at Pittodrie stands at 45,061. What was the occasion?

a	The League Championship decider against Rangers, season 1954–55	b	A League Cup tie against Celtic, season 1945–46
c	A Scottish Cup tie against Hearts, season 1953–54	d	The final game of 1954–55 against Hibs when the Dons lifted the First Division trophy

40 The biggest attendance at any game involving the Dons was at the 1937 Scottish Cup final against Celtic. What was the size of this crowd?

a	146,422	b	166,339
c	155,096	d	137,885

41 Star stats. From which club was the exceptionally gifted Pittodrie favourite Zoltan Varga signed?

a	Ferencvaros	b	Rapid Bucharest
c	Hertha Berlin	d	Red Star Belgrade

42 Who was the Dons' top scorer in season 1979–80?

a	Joe Harper	b	Dave Robb
c	Gordon Strachan	d	Steve Archibald

43 He was signed from Morton in 1969. Can you name the Aberdeen player who was to become affectionately known as 'The King'?

a	Joe Harper	b	Bobby Clark
c	Willie Miller	d	Alex McLeish

44 Nicknamed 'Cup-tie', who was Aberdeen's two-goal hero when they won the Scottish Cup in season 1969–70?

a	Arthur Graham	b	Davie Robb
c	Derek McKay	d	Jimmy Smith

45 What's the name of Aberdeen's mascot?

a	Shaggy the Sheep	b	Angus the Bull
c	Todders the Tortoise	d	Dick the Duck

46

He made 91 starts for Scotland . His last appearance was in October 1998 in the European Championship qualifier against Estonia. Who is he?

a	Alex McLeish	**b**	Doug Rougvie
c	Jim Leighton	**d**	Stuart Kennedy

47

He appeared in a Scotland jersey 34 times – twice as captain. In 1971, this Aberdeen-born defender was sold to Manchester United . Who is this superstar?

a	Stewart McKimmie	**b**	Martin Buchan
c	Duncan Shearer	**d**	Davie Robb

48

What piece of kitchen equipment was done away with in a famous Pittodrie cost-cutting exercise?

a	A kettle	**b**	A fridge
c	A dishcloth	**d**	A toaster

49

Whose biography, entitled *The King*, was published in the autumn of 2003?

a	Jim Leighton's	**b**	Joe Harper's
c	Denis Law's	**d**	Stewart Milne's

50

And, finally, Aberdeen beat Celtic 2–0 (YES!!!!!!!) at Pittodrie in December 2001. What did Dons fans throw at Celtic players during this game?

a	Pies	**b**	Coins
c	Snowballs	**d**	Flowers

'First catch yer huggis . . .'

Adapted from Mrs Beaton

Like many places, Aberdeen has foods that are unique to the area. But Aberdeen is more favoured than most in having the very best natural ingredients on its doorstep – from the north-east's organically farmed beef to the fresh fish and seafood landed each day at the city's fish market. And most Aberdonians know at least one exile from the city who dreams of waking up, wherever they are, and finding that Aitken's have opened a branch of their bakery within walking distance of their adopted home so that they can nip out and buy some newly-baked butteries.

1 **What are hairy tatties?**

a	Mashed potatoes and salt fish	b	Older potatoes, with sprouting eyes, cooked in their skins
c	A Doric name for celeriac	d	Overcooked boiled potatoes

2 **Traditionally, when would you serve bubbly jock?**

a	At a wedding feast	b	At New Year
c	At Christmas	d	At Halloween

3 **What is a howtowdie?**

a	A young chicken that's ready for the pot	b	A small Deeside cheese
c	A pudding made from raspberries and cream	d	An oatcake topped with cheese, jam and pickles

4 **What's a collop?**

a	A battered and deep-fried cockerel's foot	b	A thin slice of meat
c	A type of edible shellfish	d	A roasted oxtail

5 **What's the English name for a sybae?**

a	A spring cabbage	b	A spring chicken
c	A spring roll	d	A spring onion

6 **What is skirlie usually served with?**

a	Cooked meat, especially roast chicken or mince	**b**	Strawberries and cream
c	Whisky	**d**	Porridge

7 **And what is the main ingredient of skirlie?**

a	Oatmeal	**b**	Tatties
c	Bacon	**d**	Sausagemeat

8 **It's called skirlie because . . .?**

a	It's cooked in a skillet	**b**	The noise it makes when it's cooking sounds like skirling bagpipes
c	The chef who invented it named it after his wife, Shirley – he was useless at spelling	**d**	It makes you skirl in pain if you eat it when it's too hot

9 **What's a softie?**

a	A par-baked scone	**b**	A baker in charge of bread and other soft bakery goods
c	A doughy bread roll	**d**	An old biscuit that's lost its crispness

10 **In the north-east, they're known as 'breed'. What's the more common name for this Scottish delicacy?**

a	Oatcakes	**b**	Scotch pancakes
c	Dropped scones	**d**	Scotch eggs

11 What's the name of the world-famous breed of north-east beef cattle?

a	Buchan Brian	b	Mearns Martin
c	Aberdeen Angus	d	Deeside Donald

12 If you were 'gawn' brumullin", what would you be doing?

a	Going to a farmers' market	b	Going food shopping
c	Going to shoot partridges	d	Going to pick blackberries

13 What's a mealie pudding?

a	A sausage-shaped serving of skirlie	b	An oatmeal-based cheesecake
c	Jelly and ice cream sprinkled with toasted oatmeal	d	A helping of pudding that's so big it could equal the size of a whole meal

14 And what's another name for a mealie pudding?

a	A mealie Johnny	b	A mealie Jimmy
c	A mealie Jenny	d	A mealie Jubbly

15 What are stovies?

a	Small cookers	b	Meat-filled pancakes
c	Scones cooked on a griddle rather than in the oven	d	Potatoes, onions and leftover meat cooked together

16 **A long-standing city delicacy, what is potted hough?**

a	Cooked beef or pork from the rump served in jelly	b	Cooked beef or pork from the head served in jelly
c	Cooked beef or pork from the shin served in jelly	d	Cooked beef or pork from the rib served in jelly

17 **What is bawd bree?**

a	Sweetbreads	b	A kind of crustless loaf
c	Good meaty stock	d	Hare soup

18 **And what about partan bree?**

a	Crab soup	b	Lentil soup
c	Scotch broth	d	Grunny's soup

19 **What's a lucky tattie?**

a	A heart-shaped tattie	b	A tattie-shaped spicy sweetie with a wee plastic toy embedded in it
c	The last tattie to be taken or served from a pot	d	A tattie that's been missed at howkin' time

20 **And, if your tatties have gone through the bree, what's happened to them?**

a	They've been mashed	b	They've started sprouting
c	They've been pushed through a sieve and added to soup as a thickener	d	They've been boiled too long and are all soggy

21 Coarse, medium, fine and pinhead are grades of what?

| a | Oatmeal | b | Higher Cookery exam results |
| c | Caviar | d | Flour |

22 A buttery is also known as what?

| a | A fechtie | b | A tiffie |
| c | A rowie | d | A spattie |

23 Stappit heidies are . . .?

| a | Stuffed fish heads | b | Stuffed sheep's heads |
| c | Stuffed chicken heads | d | School head-teachers who have eaten too much |

24 What would you expect to get if you ordered cabbi claw?

| a | Scallops served in their shells | b | Salt cod served with eggs, potatoes and often parsley |
| c | Soup made from birds' feet | d | Pickled cabbage served with crabmeat |

25 Where would you go if you fancied a cappie wi' juicie?

| a | The local pub | b | The nearest Indian restaurant |
| c | The chipper (chip shop) | d | The icer (ice-cream van) |

26 And what would you get if you asked for a cappie wi' juicie?

a	An ice-cream cone with raspberry sauce	b	A bag of chips with tomato sauce
c	A whisky with ginger	d	Pakora with chilli sauce

27 Cullen skink is . . .?

a	A cheap cut of beef used to make stock for broth	b	A smoked fish soup that originated in a Buchan village
c	A thin oatmeal gruel	d	A traditional roast lizard delicacy

28 Mackie's is a favourite brand of north-east what?

a	Stovies	b	Haggis
c	Ice cream	d	Honey

29 Grunny Marshall recommends bramble jam as a cure for what?

a	Piles	b	Hiccups
c	Sore throats	d	Trapped wind

30 What is a clootie dumpling?

a	A dough ball served with stew	b	A fruit-filled pastry ball
c	A spicy steamed dessert made with dried fruit	d	A small potato ball similar to Italian gnocchi

31 And what does 'clootie' mean?

a	Cloth	b	Cloggy
c	Cloudy	d	Clove

32 What are the main ingredients of clapshot?

a	Sausage and tatties	b	Neeps and tatties
c	Mince and tatties	d	Smoked salmon and caviar

33 What is 'chuddie'?

a	Cheese	b	Chewing gum
c	The best china	d	Chardonnay

34 Which fruits would you need if you were making cranachan?

a	Raspberries	b	Pineapples
c	Kiwi fruits	d	Strawberries

35 A sheep's pluck is an essential ingredient of haggis. Which part of the animal is the pluck?

a	The liver	b	The lights
c	The heart	d	All of the above

36 And what are an animal's 'lights'?

a	Its eyes	b	Its lungs
c	Its hooves	d	Its kidneys

37 In the song, Ally Bally was greetin' for another bawbee to buy what?

a	Coulter's candy	b	Bieldside's butter
c	Miltimber's milk	d	Cults's cubbage

38 If you ordered clabbie dubhs, what would you be served with?

a	Prawns	b	Pickled onions
c	Mussels	d	Pickled eggs

39 What would you use a spurtle for?

a	Catching haggis – it's a net on a long stick	b	Keeping your porridge lump-free – it's a wooden stirring stick
c	Cooking bannocks – it's a heavy griddle	d	Cooking jam – it's a big wide pan

40 When is black bun traditionally eaten?

a	New Year	b	Easter
c	Christmas	d	Weddings

41 In Ireland, a mixture of tatties and cabbage is called colcannan. What's it called in Scotland?

a	Tumbledwhacks	b	Jumbledsmacks
c	Fumbledswipes	d	Rumbledthumps

42 A chipper in Stonehaven is said to have been the first to offer which culinary delight?

a	The haddock supper	b	The deep-fried Mars bar
c	The white pudding supper	d	The jeelyfush supper

43 Which of these is an essential ingredient of Scotch broth?

a	Asparagus	b	Whisky
c	Pearl barley	d	Oatmeal

44 How can you tell if your Scotch pie has onions in it?

a	It would have two holes in the top instead of just one	b	The pastry would be wavy round the edges
c	It would be bigger than the plain kind	d	It costs more than the plain kind

45 And, traditionally, what meat is used in Scotch pies

a	Beef	b	Chicken
c	Pork	d	Mutton

46 Dean's of Huntly are world-renowned makers of what?

a	Haggis	b	Shortbread
c	Whisky	d	Oatcakes

47 Pannanich Wells on Deeside is famous for what?

a	Being the birthplace of chef Gordon Ramsay	b	Its spring water
c	Its health spa	d	Its heather honey

48 What is brochan?

a	Cheese made in Fraserburgh	b	Fruitcake
c	Gruel with honey and butter, often served as a bedtime drink	d	Fried onions topped with eggs

49 There's a farm just off the South Deeside Road where some unusual animals are reared for food. What are they?

a	Ostriches	b	Kangaroos
c	Llamas	d	Wild boar

50 What's a tappit hen?

a	A chicken that's stuffed and ready to go in the oven	b	A chicken that's considered too wee to cook
c	A whisky decanter with a stopper in the form of a cock's comb	d	A wifie who's willing to lend you money

8 Education
A wee bittie o' it is said tae be a dangerous thing

In common with the rest of Scotland, Aberdeen has every right to be proud of its excellent and long-standing education system. The questions in this section cover higher education, the city's schools and some north-east vocabulary relating to teaching over the years.

1 In the past, what would north-east bairns have called their teachers?

a	Skittlies	b	Cardies
c	Dominies	d	Darties

2 When was Aberdeen's first university at Old Aberdeen founded?

a	1495	b	1595
c	1695	d	1795

3 What is its name?

a	Queen's College	b	King's College
c	Prince's College	d	Roger Nelson's College

4 And who was its founder?

a	Bishop John Chanonry	b	Bishop David Meston
c	Bishop William Elphinstone	d	Bishop James Dunbar

5 If somebody 'got the scud' at school, what would have happened to them?

a	Scored the lowest mark in a class test	b	Been awarded the class dunce's cap
c	Been made milk monitor for the week	d	Been belted by the teacher

6 Aberdeen's other university was founded in which year?

a	1393	b	1493
c	1593	d	1693

7 And what is its name?

a	Marischal College	b	General College
c	Colonel College	d	Sergeant College

8 And who was the principal mover in getting the 'New Town' university off the ground?

a	Fraser Burgh	b	William Huntly
c	Peter Head	d	George Keith

9 The first chair of what, in the English-speaking world, was founded at King's College in 1497?

a	Medicine	b	Philosophy
c	Mathematics	d	IT Studies

10 If the teacher told a member of the class to 'Wheesht!', what would they be asking them to do?

a	Pay attention	b	Stop talking
c	Get a move on	d	Clean the blackboard

11 Marischal College was built on the site of what?

a	A leprosy hospital	b	A Franciscan friary
c	A ruined castle	d	A prison

12 Who was the architect of the Broad Street frontage of Marischal College?

a	A Marshall Mackenzie	b	John Smith
c	Frank Matcham	d	Archibald Simpson

13 What's the name of the hall and tower in Marischal College?

a	Marshall	b	Mitchell
c	Martin	d	Meldrum

14 If you were sent home from school because you were 'flechie', what would be wrong with you?

a	You'd have the flu	b	You'd be headachy
c	You'd be feeling sick	d	You'd have fleas

15 An act of parliament of which year decreed that the city's two universities should merge?

a	1658	b	1758
c	1858	d	1958

16 How many universities in total were there in England at that time?

a	Eight	b	Ten
c	Five	d	Fighteen

17 When was Robert Gordon's Institute of Technology granted university status?

a	1992	b	1990
c	1988	d	1994

18 If you were accused of 'swicking', what would you have been doing?

a	Cheating in a test or exam	b	Chewing gum in class
c	Daydreaming	d	Talking over the teacher

19 What is the city's school of architecture called?

a	Tommy Thurso	b	Willie Wick
c	Calum Caithness	d	Scott Sutherland

20 And can you name Aberdeen's school of art?

a	Gray's	b	White's
c	Black's	d	Reid's

21 And what about the agricultural college to west of the city?

a	Chickenchuckie	b	Craibstone
c	Peterculter	d	Crabrock

22 If a pupil was practising their 'scrieving', what would they be doing?

a	Practising writing	b	Practising singing
c	Practising mental arithmetic	d	Practising spelling

23 What's the city's main library called?

a	Aberdeen City Library	b	Aberdeen Lending Library
c	Aberdeen Central Library	d	Aberdeen Library

24 On which street would you find this library?

a	Rosemount Viaduct	b	Schoolhill
c	Union Terrace	d	Skene Street

25 In days gone by, what would a teacher have used to inflict corporal punishment?

a	A hall	b	A tawse
c	A milne	d	A barratt

26 What was the name of the city's all-girls' senior secondary school?

a	Aberdeen Grammar School for Girls	b	Aberdeen High School for Girls
c	St Margaret's School for Girls	d	Albyn School for Girls

27 What's the name of this school now?

a	Cults Academy	b	Bankhead Academy
c	Aberdeen Grammar School	d	Harlaw Academy

28 And can you name this school's most famous former pupil?

a	Annie Lennox	b	Evelyn Glennie
c	Muriel Thomson	d	Dod's wife, Bunty

29 If you'd forgotten to take your 'dookers' to school, which lesson would you miss?

a	Gym – they're gym shoes	b	Maths – they're mathematical instruments
c	Art – they're colouring pencils	d	Swimming – they're swimming trunks

30 What was Aberdeen's first purpose-built comprehensive school?

a	Linksfield Academy	b	Hazlehead Academy
c	Dyce Academy	d	Northfield Academy

31 When was this comprehensive school opened?

a	1968	b	1969
c	1970	d	1971

32 And pupils from which school were moved there?

a	Aberdeen Academy	b	Aberdeen Grammar School
c	Aberdeen High School	d	Rosemount Junior Secondary School

33 Who officially opened the new school?

a	The prime minister of the day, Harold Wilson	b	The education minister of the day, Margaret Thatcher
c	The Queen	d	Alice Cooper

34 If the teacher tells you off for 'fiking', what have you been doing?

a	Telling lies	b	Fighting in the playground
c	Fidgeting	d	Copying somebody else's answers

35 People are trained to become what at Blairs College on the outskirts of Aberdeen?

a	Butlers	b	Nannies
c	Athletes	d	Roman Catholic Priests

36 What is the annual university Torcher?

a	A charity parade by city students	**b**	A bonfire to celebrate the founding of King's College
c	The end of session exams	**d**	A boring speech given by the university chancellor

37 If a pupil was 'ettling' to do something, what would they be doing?

a	Trying to do it	**b**	Avoiding it
c	Dying to do it	**d**	Hoping to do it

38 What was the name of the school opposite Robert Gordon's College?

a	Aberdeen Grammar School	**b**	Aberdeen Academy
c	Aberdeen Senior Secondary School	**d**	Aberdeen College

39 What was this school called before 1954?

a	Doon Toon School	**b**	Belmont School
c	St Nicholas School	**d**	Central School

40 Now called The Academy, what is housed in the old school today?

a	An education museum	**b**	A shopping centre with restaurants
c	An extension of Aberdeen Art Gallery	**d**	An extension of the Robert Gordon's College

41 If you were 'jouking the school', where would you be?

a	Playing arcade games at the beach	**b**	Wandering round the Bon-Accord Centre
c	At home watching *Neighbours*	**d**	Any of the above

42 When King's College first opened, its main purpose was for training people in which two professions?

a	The Church and law	**b**	Medicine and law
c	Medicine and the Church	**d**	The Church and education

43 Who became the first principal of King's College in 1514?

a	Hamish Boece	**b**	Hector Boece
c	Hubert Boece	**d**	Harold Boece

44 And, in 2003, who holds the post of principal of the University of Aberdeen?

a	Professor C Duncan Rice	**b**	Professor C Duncan Flower
c	Professor C Duncan Pasta	**d**	Professor C Duncan Chips

45 Who, in session 2003–04, is the rector of the University of Aberdeen?

a	Nick Nairn	**b**	Clarissa Dickson Wright
c	Rick Stein	**d**	Ainsley Harriot

46 If a class thought their teacher was 'fair stunkit', which of the following would they be?

a	In a bad mood	b	Sweet smelling
c	Hung-over	d	Showing no favouritism

47 What's the name of the main library of the University of Aberdeen?

a	The Queen Elizabeth II Library	b	The Bishop Elphinstone Library
c	The Queen Mother Library	d	The Earl Marischal Library

48 When King's College first opened, at what age did students normally begin their studies there?

a	Fourteen	b	Sixteen
c	Eighteen	d	Twenty-one

49 If a teacher gave a pupil an 'owergyann', what would it be?

a	An extra piece of homework	b	A piece of advice
c	A scolding	d	A detention

50 What's the name of the University of Aberdeen's student newspaper?

a	*Showie*	b	*Funcie*
c	*Flooerie*	d	*Gaudie*

9

Fitty folk, Kitty folk,
Country folk and city folk,
Folk fae Constitution Street
And folk fae Rubislaw Den –
Wallfield, Nellfield,
Mannofield and Cattofield . . .

Taken from a song written by Harry
Gordon and later revived by the
Scotland the What? team

Famous Folk

Fa div they think they are?

Folk hailing from our bonnie city or round about have made it big in almost every walk of life imaginable. Here you'll find famous sports people, MPs and MSPs rubbing shoulders with scientists, musicians, actors, poets, painters and even a ballet dancer.

1 He took the first ever photos of the moon and was appointed Astronomer Royal in1879. Who is this Aberdeen-born astronomer?

a	Sir David Gill	b	Sir Mickey Finn
c	Sir John Scale	d	Sir William Bone

2 Which architect designed the city's Music Hall?

a	Archibald Simpson	b	John Smith
c	James Matthews	d	Archibald Simpson, John Smith and James Matthews collaboratively

3 What's the real name of the self-styled Torry Quine?

a	June Imray	b	April Morrison
c	May I. Huvisduns	d	Julie Alexander

4 Who's the MSP for Aberdeen North?

a	Helen Robertson	b	Elaine Thomson
c	Alison Davidson	d	Moira Wilson

5 What's the name of the Aberdonian character in the BBC soap River City?

a	Alice	b	Roisin (pronounced Rosheen)
c	Gina	d	Scarlett

6 And can you name the actor who plays her?

a	Sally Hewitt	b	Lorraine McIntosh
c	Joyce Falconer	d	Libby McArthur

7 What's the name of the Aberdeen songstress who formed the band Eurythmics with Dave Stewart?

a	Annie Lennox	b	Patti Smith
c	Siouxsie Sioux	d	Danni Minogue

8 What was the name of the previous band she was in?

a	The Wanderers	b	The Gypsies
c	The Tourists	d	The Nomads

9 And what's the name of her most recent solo album?

a	*Annie Lennox – Nude*	b	*Annie Lennox – Bare*
c	*Annie Lennox – In the Buff*	d	*Annie Lennox – Starkers*

10 The author of *A Scots Quair*, which Scots novelist worked as a journalist on the *Aberdeen Journal* at the end of the First World War?

a	Robert Louis Stevenson	b	Lewis Grassic Gibbon
c	John Buchan	d	Arthur Conan Doyle

11 Born at Gilcomston in the city in 1848, what's the name of Aberdeen's famous female missionary?

a	Mary Slessor	b	Maggie Smith
c	Mary Sanderson	d	Maggie Moss

12 Who is the MP for Aberdeen South?

a	Susan Cadge	b	Elizabeth Proby
c	Anne Begg	d	Helen Smith

13 Known as the father of Scottish Country Dancing, he opened the city's first dance school in the eighteenth century. Can you name him?

a	Henry Sparrow	b	Charlie Drake
c	John Parrot	d	Francis Peacock

14 What's the name of the poet who, in 1357, became archdeacon of St Machar's Cathedral?

a	John MacIntosh	b	John Wellington
c	John Barbour	d	John Burberry

15 What's the name of the artist famous for his Aberdeen cityscapes?

a	Jim Young	b	Eric Auld
c	Fred Elder	d	William Younger

16 The first Photographer Royal was an Aberdonian. Who was he?

a	Thomas Jefferson Wilson	b	Abraham Lincoln Wilson
c	George Washington Wilson	d	George Dubya Wilson

17 Who is the MP for Aberdeen Central?

a	Frank Doran	b	Albert Egon
c	Dean Francis	d	Martin Graham

18 Born in Aberdeen in 1965, which profoundly deaf person became a world-famous percussionist and composer?

a	Rick Allen	b	Ringo Star
c	Mick Fleetwood	d	Evelyn Glennie

19 Can you name the Aberdeen-born Olympic gold-medallist swimmer?

a	David Wilkie	b	Duncan Goodhew
c	Mark Spitz	d	Anita Lonsbrough

20 For which event did this person win their gold medal?

a	The 200m freestyle	b	The 200m butterfly
c	The 200m backstroke	d	The 200m breaststroke

21 And at which games did they win it

a	Mexico, 1968	b	Munich, 1972
c	Montreal, 1976	d	Moscow, 1980

22 He was most famous for playing Dr Cameron in *Dr Finlay's Casebook*. Who was this actor who was born in Aberdeen in 1907?

a	Bill Simpson	b	Andrew Cruickshank
c	David Snoddy	d	Jim Mullen

23 Born at Craigmyle, just outside the city, in 1814, what title did Sir Walter Scott bestow on magician John Henry Anderson?

a	The Great Wizard of the North	b	The Caledonian Conjuror
c	The Scottish Sorcerer	d	The Magician of the Mearns

24 Famous as one of 'The Goodies', he was born in Aberdeen in 1943. What's his name?

a	Graeme Garden	b	Bill Oddie
c	Tim Brooke-Taylor	d	Michael Palin

25 Who's the MSP for Aberdeen Central?

a	Lyle MacIntosh	b	Lennox MacKenzie
c	Laughlin MacLeod	d	Lewis MacDonald

26 Educated at the University of Aberdeen, he became a Northsound DJ before heading for shows on Radio 1 and venturing into TV. Who is he?

a	Mike Reid	**b**	John Peel
c	Nicky Campbell	**d**	Kid Jensen

27 Brought up in Kintore, can you name this choreographer and dancer who was born in Aberdeen in 1962?

a	Michael Clark	**b**	James Farmer
c	John Baker	**d**	Billy Elliot

28 What was the name of the first general manager of the BBC? He was born in Stonehaven in 1889.

a	William Garland	**b**	John Reith
c	Peter Posy	**d**	Reginald Bosanquet

29 One of Scotland's top businessmen, he's also chairman of Aberdeen FC. Who is he?

a	Owen Rugg	**b**	Carr Pitt
c	Perry Wigg	**d**	Stewart Milne

30 Can you name the fiddler and composer of fiddle music, known as 'The Strathspey King', who was born at Banchory in 1843?

a	James Scott Skinner	**b**	John Scott Butcher
c	William Scott Tanner	**d**	David Scott Dyer

31 Who's the MSP for Aberdeen South?

a	Nicol Stephen	**b**	Steven Nicol
c	Travis Bickle	**d**	Tommy Tickle

32 He lived in Forres and was one half of the folk duo The Corries. Can you name him?

a	Pete Davidson	**b**	Steve Paterson
c	Roy Williamson	**d**	Bob Robertson

33 And what is the name of the other member of The Corries?

a	Robbie Green	**b**	Bobby Black
c	Jimmy Reid	**d**	Ronnie Browne

34 Who is world champion squash player who was born in Inverurie in 1973?

a	Paul Nicholson	**b**	Peter Nicol
c	Philip Nichols	**d**	Spiro Nicolaisen

35 He was born in Aberdeen in 1888 and became a popular comic film actor. Who was he?

a	Will Hay	**b**	Fred Straw
c	Gunter Grass	**d**	Al Bran

36 Which Aberdeen-based golfer won the 1999 Open Golf Championship at Carnoustie?

a	Eugene Dadi	b	Ross Ferry
c	Charles Berry	d	Paul Lawrie

37 Who's the MP for Aberdeen North?

a	Robbie Savage	b	Alan Rough
c	Sid Vicious	d	Malcolm Savage

38 Born in 1777 just outside Stonehaven, what was Robert Barclay Allardice famous for?

a	Long distance walking	b	Long distance swimming
c	Long distance yodelling	d	Long distance semaphoring

39 Which comedian, the self-styled 'Laird of Inversnecky', was born in the city in 1893?

a	Lex McLean	b	Will Fyfe
c	Harry Gordon	d	Eddie Izzard

40 Which BBC Scotland sports presenter is an Aberdonian?

a	Stuart Cosgrove	b	Richard Gordon
c	Tam Cowan	d	Dougie Vipond

41 Sir Ian Wood is Chairman and Chief Executive of the John Wood Group plc. He graduated with a first class honours degree in which subject?

a	Psychology	b	Business Management
c	Engineering	d	Veterinary Medicine

42 What's the name of the famous poet who was born in the London but moved to the city shortly after his birth in 1788?

a	Samuel Taylor Coleridge	b	Percy Bysse Shelley
c	John Keats	d	George Gordon

43 How is this poet better known?

a	George Herbert	b	George Harrison
c	Lord Byron	d	George Bernard Shaw

44 Lady Caroline Lamb famously described him as . . .?

a	Handsome, amusing and very, very sexy	b	Mad, bad and dangerous to know
c	Mad, sad and really quite ridiculous	d	Plook-faced and rather smelly

45 What's the name of the BBC news reporter who was raised in Aberdeen?

a	Eric Crockart	b	Kate Adie
c	Jeremy Bowen	d	Margaret Gilmore

46 Who was the Fraserburgh-born man who founded the Japanese shipbuilding firm that became Mitsubishi?

a	Thomas Blake Glover	**b**	William Brown Shoemaker
c	James White Tanner	**d**	John Reid Cooper

47 This man is believed to have been the model for a character in which Puccini opera?

a	*La Bohème*	**b**	*Madama Butterfly*
c	*Tosca*	**d**	*Manon Lescaut*

48 He was born in Ballater in 1854 and became known as the father of modern town-planning. Can you name him?

a	Sir Patrick Spens	**b**	Sir Patrick Steptoe
c	Sir Patrick Geddes	**d**	Sir Patrick Moore

49 Born in Braemar in 1945, can you name the folk singer who was one half of the duo Peter and Gordon?

a	Peter Asher	**b**	Gordon Miller
c	Peter Piper	**d**	Gordon Waller

50 One of triplets, what's the name of the Aberdeen professional woman golfer?

a	Muriel Thomson	**b**	Margaret Anderson
c	Mary Davidson	**d**	Mandy Harrison

10

Miscellaneous
A rugbug o' ither stuff

'All human life is here.'
News of the World

We'll be straying outside the city limits sometimes for this bittie so, if you've got a teuchter on your phone-a-friend list, you'll do well.

1 One of Scotland's biggest prisons is in which north-east town?

| a | Stonehaven | b | Banff |
| c | Muchalls | d | Peterhead |

2 What's the name of Aberdeen's prison?

| a | Craiginches | b | Craigfoot |
| c | Craigyard | d | Craigmile |

3 Which of the city's statues was described as 'not a man in a chair but a chair with a man in it'?

| a | William Wallace's | b | Robert Burns's |
| c | Prince Albert's | d | Sir Alex Ferguson's |

4 Which north-east town holds the annual Ythan Raft Race?

| a | Ellon | b | Fyvie |
| c | Methlick | d | Newburgh |

5 Where, in the north-east, is there a new-age commune?

| a | Forres | b | Elgin |
| c | Craigellachie | d | Findhorn |

6 When was Scotland's oldest lighthouse built?

a	1767	**b**	1787
c	1807	**d**	1827

7 And this lighthouse is in which north-east town?

a	Macduff	**b**	Banff
c	Fraserburgh	**d**	Peterhead

8 Originally, what fuelled the light of this lighthouse?

a	Whale oil	**b**	Candles
c	Paraffin	**d**	Charcoal

9 The area around Inverurie is called the Garioch. How do you pronounce this?

a	Garry-ock (as in cock)	**b**	Garry-och (as in och aye)
c	Greeosh (as in brioche, the French bread)	**d**	Gearay (as in gear ray)

10 Which town holds a Festival of Traditional Music and Song each June?

a	Turriff	**b**	Huntly
c	Mintlaw	**d**	Keith

11 Lossiemouth is the birthplace of which former prime minister?

a	Harold Wilson	**b**	Alec Douglas Home
c	Ramsay MacDonald	**d**	Harold Macmillan

12 Which north-east town is renowned for its marble?

a	Gardenstown	**b**	Portsoy
c	Pennen	**d**	Cullen

13 And marble from this town was used in the construction of which famous building?

a	The Palace of Westminster	**b**	The Palace of Holyroodhouse
c	The Palace of Versailles	**d**	The Palace aff Bridge Street

14 Who became manager of Aberdeen Football Club in May 1999?

a	Ebbe Skovdahl	**b**	Paul Hegarty
c	Alex Miller	**d**	Roy Aitken

15 And who took over from him in December 2002?

a	Steve Archibald	**b**	Steve Tosh
c	Steve Austin	**d**	Steve Paterson

16 What's the name of the famous north-east trout fishery?

a	Glen of Rothes	b	Valley of the Dover Soles
c	Strath of Fochabers	d	Vale of Leven

17 If you catch one of this fishery's tagged fish, what prize can you claim?

a	A can of Irn-Bru	b	A tin of shortbread
c	A half bottle of malt whisky	d	A kilted doll

18 One of the largest agricultural shows is held in which Aberdeenshire town?

a	Oldmeldrum	b	Torphins
c	Pitmedden	d	Turriff

19 According to the song, where does the floo-er o' a' the bonnie lasses bide?

a	Banchory-o	b	Fyvie-o
c	The Garioch-o	d	Fourie-o

20 Where is the north-east's unofficial naturist beach?

a	Balmedie	b	Collieston
c	Newburgh	d	Cove

21 What's the name of the Hazlehead riding school?

a	Wheatfield	b	Strawberryfields
c	Paddyfield	d	Hayfield

22 Which north-east town is home to Scotland's Lighthouse Museum?

a	Fraserburgh	b	Peterhead
c	Buckie	d	Cruden Bay

23 Where, in the city centre, would you go if you wanted a game of tenpin bowling?

a	Rose Street	b	Summer Street
c	George Street	d	Allan Street

24 What's the name of the cartoon couple in the *Evening Express*?

a	Dod 'n' Bunty	b	Charlie 'n' Ina
c	Willie 'n' Annie	d	Torquil 'n' Camilla

25 What's the Boddam Coo?

a	A Buchan cow that produced a record amount of milk	b	A foghorn
c	A Buchan cow that produced a record number of calves	d	The sound a Buchan doo makes

26 Which former punk rocker wrote a book about stone circles, many of which are in Aberdeenshire?

a	Joey Ramone	b	Jonathan Richman
c	Johnny Rotten	d	Julian Cope

27 What's the name of the children's theme park off the South Deeside Road?

a	Storybook Glen	b	Happy Valley
c	Sleepy Hollow	d	Dingly Dell

28 Which contemporary author claimed that magic was 'not living in Aberdeen anymore'?

a	Ian Rankin	b	Christopher Brookmyre
c	J K Rowling	d	Irvine Welsh

29 What activity would you go to Glenshee or the Lecht for?

a	Winter sports	b	Water sports
c	Birdwatching	d	Trainspotting

30 Which of the city's golf courses holds an annual pro-cel-am tournament?

a	Murcar	b	Royal Aberdeen
c	Deeside	d	Auchmill

31 What's the small blue tower at the Holburn Street end of Justice Mill Lane for?

a	It's an early form of a keep-left sign	**b**	It's a ventilator for sewer gas
c	It's all that's left of a public toilet	**d**	It's all that's left of a fountain

32 Apart from a castle, what's a balmoral?

a	A waistcoat	**b**	An overcoat
c	A jumper	**d**	A brimless hat

33 What's the name of the hands-on education centre on Constitution Street?

a	Stratosphere	**b**	Biosphere
c	Atmosphere	**d**	Troposphere

34 What's the name of the model farm near Lumphanan?

a	Noah's Ark Model Farm	**b**	Ass's Jaw Model Farm
c	Moses' Basket Model Farm	**d**	Jacob's Ladder Model Farm

35 Which north-east town hosts the Scottish Traditional Boat Festival in June each year?

a	Rosehearty	**b**	Portsoy
c	Inverallochy	**d**	Strichen

36 What's the name of AFC's internet supporters' football team?

a	Baaaacelona	b	Athletico Madram
c	Inter Ma Lamb	d	Benficbaaaa

37 What's the name of the Aberdeenshire road that's frequently closed because of heavy snow?

a	Cock Bridge to Tomintoul	b	Bridge of Don to Ellon
c	Westhill to Dunecht	d	Bieldside to Kingswells

38 Which town is Deeside Gliding Club nearest to?

a	Aboyne	b	Kincardine O'Neil
c	Banchory	d	Ballater

39 What's the monument at the end of the North Pier in Fittie called?

a	Scary's Monument	b	Clarty's Monument
c	Mingy's Monument	d	Scarty's Monument

40 And what is the purpose of the monument?

a	It's a vent for a sewer outlet	b	It marks the point where a fishing boat sank
c	It's a memorial to drowned fishermen	d	It was a lookout tower

41 What's the name of the farm at Nigg that specialises in rare breeds of sheep and cattle?

a	Uppies	b	Sideyweys
c	Doonies	d	Inside-ooties

42 Which city church has the largest set of bells of any church in the Britain?

a	Rubislaw	b	Queen's Cross
c	St Nicholas	d	Beechgrove

43 And how many bells does it have?

a	48	b	37
c	96	d	25

44 What's the name of Aberdeen's airport?

a	Stoneywood	b	Bucksburn
c	Dyce	d	Potterton

45 Which Shakespearean character is said to have been killed at Lumphanan in Aberdeenshire?

a	King Lear	b	Othello
c	Cymbeline	d	Macbeth

46 In which Aberdeenshire village is there a woollen mill museum?

a	Dunecht	b	Garlogie
c	Torphins	d	Monymusk

47 What's the name of the New-Pitsligo-born fashion designer?

a	Maurice Gibb	b	Robin Gibb
c	Bill Gibb	d	Barry Gibb

48 What's a 'poor-oot'?

a	Money the father of a bride throws to local bairns	b	Closing time at Charlie's
c	A spell of heavy rain	d	A tirade of abuse

49 What's the name of the cliffs just north of Cruden Bay?

a	Bullers of Boddam	b	Bullers of Burnhaven
c	Bullers of Banff	d	Bullers of Buchan

50 And what does 'bullers' mean?

a	Rushing waters	b	Eroded cliffs
c	Noisy seabirds	d	Scary cliff paths

THE ANSWERS

1 Geography

1 How many Aberdeens are there in the world?
c **Just over 30**

2 What is the name of the Granite City's huge quarry?
a **Rubislaw**

3 And what's the huge gothic granite building in the city centre called?
c **Marischal College**

4 Near the Castlegate, there's a narrow lane called Lodge Walk. How did this wee street get its name?
c **It led to the back entrance of a hotel where Masonic meetings were held**

5 What's the local name for the road junction at the top of George Street?
c **Split-the-Win'**

6 Whose statue stands across the road from His Majesty's Theatre?
d **William Wallace's**

7 And whose statue sits on the grassy area just behind this?
b **Prince Albert's**

8 There's a statue of Queen Victoria at Queen's Cross. What's the name of the church the regal gaze looks out on?
a **Rubislaw**

9 In the 1820s, the arches of the Mercat Cross at the Castlegate were boarded up and a door was constructed to allow it to function as what?
b **The city's main post office**

10 The Mercat Cross has a sculpture of what on top of it?
c **A unicorn**

11 A statue of which poet stands in the grounds of Aberdeen Grammar School?
c **Lord Byron**

12 Somewhere in the city, there are sculpted reliefs of a naked woman riding a stylised horse. Called *The Spirit of the Winds*, where can you see them?
a **Above the entrances to the housing block, Rosemount Square**

13 Where is Provost Ross's house?
b **Shiprow**

14 And Provost Ross's house now forms part of which museum?
c **The Maritime Museum**

15 The city's cathedral in Old Aberdeen is named after which saint?
b **St Machar**

16 If you had arranged to meet somebody at the 'Monkey House', where would you expect to see them?
a **At the Commercial Union offices on the corner of Union Terrace**

17 Which of the city's parks boasts a huge maze?
b **Hazlehead**

18 There's stream that runs through the centre of the city, sometimes disappearing underground. What's its name?
c **Denburn**

19 A lighthouse overlooks Balnagask Golf Course. What's its name?

a **Girdleness**

20 Who designed the lighthouse?

a **Robert Stevenson Sr**

21 Where is the city's Catholic cathedral?

d **Huntly Street**

22 And what's its name?

b **St Mary's Cathedral**

23 Which of Aberdeen's housing estates is named after a Netherlands town?

c **Mastrick**

24 Approximately how long is Union Street?

b **A mile**

25 What's the name of the hospital behind His Majesty's Theatre?

a **Woolmanhill**

26 What would you find next to Robert Gordon's College?

a **Aberdeen Art Gallery**

27 In Union Terrace, there's a statue of Burns holding something in his hand. Periodically stolen, what is it?

b **A flower**

28 Down at the seafront, there used to be a large red brick building. Demolished in the 1960s, what was its purpose?

b **Public swimming baths**

29 The Bon-Accord Baths in Justice Mill Lane are also known as what?

a **The Uptoon Baths**

30 Erected in 1290, what's the name of the bridge over the Don in Old Aberdeen?

b **The Brig o' Balgownie**

31 In which of the city's park can you find a garden for blind and disabled people?

c **Victoria**

32 What's the name of the now disused theatre that stands on Guild Street, along from the bus and railway stations?

a **The Tivoli**

33 What's the name of the extension to the Aberdeen Art Gallery?

b **Cowdray Hall**

34 What used to stand on Great Northern Road between Ashgrove Road and the Northern Hotel?

d **A mart**

35 What's the name of the long low hill down at The Links?

b **Broad Hill**

36 What's the dilapidated bridge across the Dee at Cults called?

b **Shakkin' Briggie**

37 Whose statue stands on the rocks above the Leuchar Burn at Peterculter?

a **Rob Roy McGregor's**

38 What was the name of the hotel in Cults that was destroyed in a tragic gas explosion?

c **The Royal Darroch**

39 How many roads lead off the massive Mounthooly roundabout?

b **Five – Mounthooly, West North Street, Gallowgate, Hutcheon Street and Causewayend**

40 You've decided to go to Rose Street for a kebab after a few drinks at The College. How do you get there?

a **You cross the road, head up Union Street and take the first left**

41 Where would you find Aberdeen's famous hostelry, Ma Cameron's (assuming you hadn't already been to The College)?

a **Little Belmont Street**

42 A petition saved which of the city centre's bars from demolition? Clue – it has a famously long bar and serves some of the best stovies in town.

b **The Prince of Wales**

43 What's the popular name of the small port and fishing village beside North Pier?

b **Fittie**

44 For many years, the city's main post office occupied an impressive granite building on which street?

b **Crown Street**

45 Where is the annual Offshore Europe shindig held?

b **Aberdeen Exhibition and Conference Centre**

46 Where are the Winter Gardens?

a **The Duthie Park**

47 We've met two of the city's cathedrals. What's the name of the third one?

a **St Andrew's**

48 And which famous US citizen visited this cathedral in his youth?

a **John F Kennedy**

49 What's the defence site at Torry called?

b **The Torry Battery**

50 With its streams, ponds and rustic bridges, what's the name of the small park on Viewfield Road?

a **Johnston Gardens**

2 History

1 What is the population of Aberdeen believed to have been around the year 1200?
c **3,000**

2 When was Aberdeen granted a royal charter to give it burgh status?
b **1179**

3 Who granted the charter for this?
b **William the Lion**

4 Who is the patron saint of Aberdeen?
a **St Nicholas**

5 During the Middle Ages, Aberdeen did business with members of which trading alliance?
a **Hanseatic League**

6 And when was Old Aberdeen officially incorporated as part of the city?
d **1890**

7 What is the city's motto?
c **Bon Accord**

8 Union Street got its name in honour of what?
a **The Treaty of Union between Britain and Ireland**

9 Which two creatures appear on Aberdeen's coat of arms?
b **Two leopards**

10 There are three towers on the coat of arms. What do they represent?
d **The three hills the city is built on**

11 Which street was originally intended to be the city's main street?
b **Broad Street**

12 In which year was the Trinity Centre opened?
d **1985**

13 When was the International Youth Festival first held?
b **1973**

14 When was the Music Hall opened?
b **1822**

15 What, according to the first census of 1801, was the population of the city?
a **27,000**

16 When did Aberdeen get its first railway connection?
b **1850**

17 And when did the first steam trawlers appear?
c **1882**

18 In which year was St Nicholas House built?
a **1967**

19 Who granted the city charters in recognition of Aberdonians' help against the English in the Scottish Wars of Independence?
b **Robert the Bruce**

20 He also bestowed one of his royal hunting forests on the city. What was its name?
a **Stocket**

21 The forest subsequently became known as what?
d **Freedom Lands**

22 Sixty-seven stones mark the inner boundaries of these lands. What are they called?
b March Stones

23 As well as the royal hunting forest, funds were also donated for the building of what?
b The Brig o' Balgownie

24 Which English king destroyed huge parts of Aberdeen in 1337 in retaliation for this help?
b Edward II

25 What's the name of the much-moved wellhead, first erected in 1708, that now stands at the Castlegate?
a The Mannie Well

26 By 1861, the census showed the population had risen to . . .?
d 74,000

27 Which town is thought to be the oldest on Deeside?
d Kincardine O'Neil

28 Where in the city was a leprosy hospital founded in 1363?
a Spital Hill

29 When was the last recorded case of leprosy in the city?
b 1600s

30 In which year was Aberdeen struck by a typhoid epidemic?
c 1964

31 Who was the Chief Medical Officer of Health at the time?
d Dr Ian MacQueen

32 The city was quarantined for how long?
b Nearly a month

33 What was identified as the source of the outbreak?
b Corned beef from Argentina

34 What's the name of the battle Robert the Bruce fought near Inverurie against Red Comyn in 1308?
d Battle of Burra

35 One of Scotland's bloodiest battles was also fought near Inverurie – this time in 1411. Can you name it?
a Battle of Harlaw

36 Legend has it that whose leg is immured in St Machar's Cathedral?
a William Wallace's

37 What went on at the traditional feein' markets?
c Agricultural workers were hired

38 When were the biannual feein' markets held?
b Whitsun and Martinmas

39 How many folk were living in the city by the time of the 1911 census?
a 164,000

40 What, originally, was a bothy?
d A hut where unmarried male farm workers lived

41 In 1664, which royalist plundered the city?
b Marquis of Montrose

42 The perpetrator of this raid was later executed. Which part of his body was sent to the city as proof of his death?
a His arm

43 In the nineteenth century, Aberdeen's shipyards were world famous for the clippers they built to transport what?
b Tea

44 When were electric trams introduced in the city?
a 1894

45 When did the Cairngorm funicular railway first start running?
d 2001

46 How did the Grampian Mountains get their name?
b From the Latin name of a Roman battle site

47 What's the name of Aberdeen's Museum of Civic History?
a Tolbooth Museum

48 What was the Wardhouse that forms part of this museum?
c A jail

49 In the museum you can see something called a 'maiden'. What was it used for?
a Executions – it's a guillotine

50 Currently, what's the population of the city?
a About 215,000

3 Language

1 What's a 'quine' or 'quinie'?
b **A girl**

2 And what's a 'loun' or 'lounie'?
a **A boy**

3 What's a 'feel gype'?
d **A really stupid person**

4 If you were 'bleezin'', what state would you be in?
c **Very drunk**

5 If you 'cowp' something, what do you do to it?
b **Knock it over**

6 If someone's 'awa' fur a daunder', where are they?
c **Taking a stroll**

7 If someone said 'Hiv ye hid yer eenfu'?', what would they asking you?
a **To stop staring**

8 If you say you have a 'youkie doup', what have you got?
b **An itchy bum**

9 When would you call on the services of a 'howdie'?
a **When a baby's about to be born – she's a midwife**

10 What do you get if you get a 'fleg'?
b **A shock**

11 What should you avoid doing with a person who's known as a 'claik'?
b **Telling them a secret – a 'claik' is a gossip**

12 If someone asked 'Far d'ye bide?', what would they want to know?
c **Where you stay**

13 If you asked someone for a 'bosie', what would you want?
b **A cuddle**

14 If someone said to you 'Dinna fash yersel'.', what would they be advising you to do?
d **Not to worry**

15 Where would you wear your 'beets'?
a **On your feet – they're boots**

16 Somebody greets you with 'Fit like 'i day, min?'. What are they saying?
b **How are you today, sir?**

17 Someone asks how you are and you reply 'Ah'm jist tyauvin' (pronounced chavvin) awa'.'. What does this mean?
a **I'm struggling on**

18 If someone's face is described as being like 'a skelpit erse', what does it resemble?
b **A smacked bottom**

19 If your mum shouts at you for 'pitting dubs on 'i clean fleer', what have you done?
c **Made the floor all muddy**

20 If you're 'speirin'', what are you doing?
b **Asking someone questions**

21 If you answered the door in your 'semmit', what would you be wearing?
c **A vest**

22 Which of the following best describes a bairn that is 'thrawn'?
d Naughty and difficult to control

23 Which of these means empty?
a Teem

24 What's a 'tourie'?
b A woolly hat with a pom-pom

25 If a cat's 'raxin' oot', what's it doing?
b Having a good stretch

26 Who would wear 'dungars'?
a A workman – they're overalls

27 If someone asked you for a 'spunk', what would they be wanting?
d A match or a light for their fag

28 What are you doing to the tatties if you're 'breein' them'?
c Draining them

29 If somebody asked you to do something 'ivnoo', when would they expect you to do it?
a Straightaway

30 If a person 'hirples', what do they do?
a Walk with a limp

31 What are 'chuckies'?
b Granite chips

32 If something's 'foostie', what's wrong with it?
c It's rotten

33 If you heard somebody say 'Gyaaaaaaaads!', what would they be expressing?
b Disgust

34 If someone asked you 'Fit's adee?', what would they mean?
a What's the matter?

35 If somebody's 'a bittie dottilt', what are they?
b A little confused

36 What's a 'bachle'?
a An old worn-out shoe

37 If you were wearing 'gey nippit brikks', what would you have on?
d Trousers that are on the tight side

38 If you told somebody 'Ah'm gan tae a pluntin' 'i day', what would you mean?
b I'm attending a funeral today

39 Who would wear a 'hippen'?
b A baby – it's a nappy

40 If someone is 'foggin', what are they?
c Wealthy

41 If somebody said you were 'grippy', would you be pleased?
c No – it means mean

42 If someone gave you a 'kittle', what would you do?
c Laugh – it's a tickle

43 What's a 'cuttie'?
c A short tobacco pipe

44 What do you do to somebody if you 'clype' on them?
a Tell tales about them

45 What does a 'scaffie' do for a living?
d Sweeps the streets

46 What's a 'redd-up'?
a A session of cleaning and tidying

47 If you bend back your finger and hurt it, what have you done to it?
d Staived it

48 If you were caught 'chorin'', what would you have been doing?
c Stealing

49 Where would a 'chunty' be kept?
a Under the bed – it's a chamber pot

50 How would you describe a room that's dusty?
b Stoorie

4 Work

1 Established in Aberdeen in 1136, what is Britain's oldest business?
d Aberdeen Harbour Board

2 It was founded in Aberdeen in 1498 and is still in business today. Can you name the world's oldest recorded transport company?
b The Shore Porters Society

3 The *Aberdeen Journal*, a forerunner of the *Press and Journal*, is one of Britain's oldest newspapers. In which year was it first printed?
a 1748

4 Robert Davidson of Aberdeen worked in the early nineteenth century developing something we all take for granted today. What?
c Electric motors

5 What were the surnames of the owners of the textile mill at Granholm?
a Crombie and Knowles

6 What kind of business was Isaac Benzies?
c A department store

7 What was the name of the sporting goods store that formerly stood on George Street?
a The Rubber Shop

8 From 1903 to 1972, what did Cocky Hunter's sell?
d Bric-a-brac and second-hand stuff

9 And what is Cocky Hunter's nowadays?
b A city centre pub
d Any untidy place

10 A long-time favourite with Aberdonians, what's the name of the restaurant just past Union Bridge?
a Victoria

11 The restaurant is above which of the city's jeweller's shops?
d Jamieson and Carry

12 What are silver darlings?
b Herring
c A swanky seafood restaurant

13 What were Fifies and Zulus?
b Types of herring fishing boats

14 Which of these is a common way of fishing for herring?
c Drift netting

15 Fishermen believe that catching which fish at sea is unlucky?
b Salmon

16 On which day of the week did whalers never set sail because it was thought to be unlucky?
a Friday

17 And which kind of a person is thought to bring bad luck to fishing boats?
c A clergyman

18 Some trawlers use long vertically hanging nets called . . .?
c Seine nets

19 What, in arable farming, was the 'guidman's grund'?
b An area left unplanted to appease the devil

20 Which rock is most commonly seen on the Earth's surface?
d Granite

21 What type of rock is granite?
a Igneous

22 What's the name for the glittery bitties in granite?
b Mica

23 640,000 cubic feet of Aberdeen granite went into building of what?
c The Forth Rail Bridge

24 Where is John Fyffe's Paradise Quarry?
b Kemnay

25 In which decade did Rubislaw Quarry close?
a 1970s

26 From which north-east town does the delicious Rizza's ice cream hail?
d Huntly

27 Officially, when did North Sea oil first come ashore?
d 1975

28 From which oilfield did it flow?
a Forties

29 Who inaugurated its flow?
b The Queen

30 And where did the oil come ashore?
c Cruden Bay

31 What is the name of famous oil industry firefighter?
c 'Red' Adair

32 In 2002, the biggest discovery of North Sea oil in over a decade was made. In which field?
a Buzzard

33 What's the name of the Roger Moore character in the oil rig thriller movie *North Sea Hijack*?
c ffolkes

34 What has been businessman Bob Farquhar's contribution to the North Sea oil industry?
b Supply of portable toilets

35 What's a labourer on an oilrig called?
a A roustabout

36 First produced in an Aberdeen textile mill, what is a Crombie?
a A cashmere overcoat

37 What's the name of the north-east village where the food-producer Baxter's is based?
d Fochabers

38 What was the name of the Hatton-based biscuit producers?
a Simmers

39 When was Aberdeen's first shipyard founded?
c 1753

40 Which was the last Aberdeen shipyard to close?
a Hall Russell

41 Which three ingredients are needed to make whisky?
a Water, yeast and barley

42 What is the name of the sugary liquid produced at the start of the whisky-making process?
b Wort

43 In which Banffshire town is Glenfiddich whisky produced?
d Dufftown

44 Where, in the north-east, is Walker's shortbread produced?
a Aberlour

45 What's the name of the paper mill at Stoneywood?
b Arjo Wiggins

46 What was Lawsons of Dyce famous for producing?
c Sausages

47 Which famous architect designed the Aberdeen Business School at Garthdee?
a Sir Norman Foster

48 Where is Thainstone Mart, the most modern livestock market in Europe?
c Kintore

49 Which Aberdeenshire company is famous for its milk and ice-cream production?
a Mackies

50 Aberdeen's is the busiest in the world. Aberdeen's what?
b Heliport

5 Culture

1 Aberdeen has won the Britain in Bloom a record number of times. How many?

a **Ten**

2 September 1896 saw a significant first for Aberdeen's Music Hall. What was it?

b **It screened 18 short films over three days and was, therefore, the city's first cinema**

3 What type of classical columns can be seen at the front of the Music Hall?

a **Ionic**

4 Where, traditionally, is the amateur Christmas pantomime held?

d **Aberdeen Arts Centre**

5 And which theatre group puts on the panto?

b **The Attic Theatre Group**

6 Is this amateur panto generally considered to be better than its professional rival at HMT?

a **Oh, yes, it is**

c **Aye, iv coorse it is**

7 What's the name of the annual market held at the Castlegate?

b **Timmer Market**

8 And what was the original purpose of this market?

c **The sale of wooden goods**

9 How many official twin towns does Aberdeen have?

a **Five**

10 What's the name of the festival held in July and August each year?

d **Aberdeen International Youth Festival**

11 What's the name of the venue on West North Street?

d **The Lemon Tree**

12 His Majesty's Theatre is about to be twinned with another HMT. Where is it?

a **Perth, Australia**

13 Which north-east town is known as 'The Bloo Toon'?

b **Peterhead**

14 What was the Tivoli Theatre formerly known as?

c **His Majesty's Opera House**

15 What's the name of the National Trust gardens near Ellon?

b **Pitmedden**

16 The year 2003 saw Aberdeen FC celebrate its centenary. What sporting event also reached its one-hundredth anniversary in that year?

c **The Tour de France**

17 Forvie Nature Reserve is close to which town?

a **Newburgh**

18 Which hill would you climb to reach the peak known as Mither Tap?

d **Bennachie**

19 Which Aberdeenshire town holds a Doric festival in October each year?

a **Inverurie**

20 Which French town is Aberdeen twinned with?

c **Clermont-Ferrand**

21 Slains Castle is thought to be the site that inspired the creation of which literary character?

b Count Dracula

22 Which north-east castle was used as the backdrop for Zeffirelli's film version of *Hamlet*?

d Dunnotter Castle

23 Attended by the royal family, what is the name best-known Highland Games?

a The Braemar Gathering

24 The modern games were first held in 1832 but who is said to have inaugurated them many years before that?

c Malcolm Ceann-mor

25 Where in the north east is there a transport museum?

b Alford

26 What's the name of the comedy team, popular in the 1970s and 1980s, whose sketches and songs were in Doric?

a Scotland the What?

27 Which of the following was not a member of this comedy team?

b Douglas Kynoch

28 What, according to the Scotland the What? team, is a 'futret'?

d A ferret

29 And they suggest which of the following is how 'futret' should be spelt?

d F E R R E T

30 Which German town is Aberdeen twinned with?

c Regensburg

31 Which north-east personality presents Radio Scotland's weekly country dance music show?

c Robbie Shepherd

32 There used to be a small zoo in the city. Where was it?

b Hazlehead Park

33 What do people flock to the Falls of Feuch at Banchory to see?

c Salmon leaping upstream

34 Where in Aberdeen is the Gordon Highlanders Museum?

a Just off Queen's Road

35 What can unexpectedly be found in the Mannofield area of the city?

b A cricket ground

36 What exciting activity can you take part in at Kaimhill?

b Skiing on the dry ski slope

37 Which of the actors in *The Bill* was born in Aberdeen?

d Jeff Stewart

38 And which character does he play?

a Reg Hollis

39 While Robbie Shepherd was on holiday in 2003, who presented his *The Reel Blend* Scottish country dance music radio programme?

b Cameron Stout

40 Which Norwegian town is Aberdeen twinned with?

a   Stavanger

41 Who's the Aberdonian who presents the Radio 3 arts programme *Night Waves*?

d   Isabel Hilton

42 Which north-east town has an annual Hogmanay Fireball Festival?

a   Stonehaven

43 Which town in Belarus is Aberdeen twinned with?

a   Gomel

44 When did Grampian TV first appear on our tellies?

b   1961

45 Which north-east town is known as 'The Broch'?

c   Fraserburgh

46 What's the name of the walk that runs from Bennachie to Rhynie?

a   The West Gordon Way

47 Just north of Pitmedden, there's a house that was built by the second Earl of Aberdeen in 1731. What's its name?

a   Haddo House

48 Haddo House is famous for what?

d   Its opera company

49 Which town in Zimbabwe is Aberdeen twinned with?

b   Bulawayo

50 Where is the north-east's Agricultural Heritage Centre?

a   Aden Country Park

6 Football

1 He never played for the Dons but Denis Law is undoubtedly Aberdeen's most famous footballing son. At which club did he spend most of his career?
c **Manchester United**

2 Which boys' club did Denis play for?
a **Aberdeen Lads' Club**

3 And which English club first signed the young Lawman?
b **Huddersfield Town**

4 Law became the first £100,000 footballer when he signed for which Italian club?
a **Torino**

5 How many caps did Denis Law win for Scotland?
d **55**

6 And how many international goals did Law score to make him Scotland's joint top scorer?
a **30**

7 Denis Law shares this record with . . .?
d **Kenny Dalglish**

8 Which club was the last one to have Denis on its books?
a **Manchester City**

9 And, in the twilight of his playing career, which team's relegation was sealed by a Denis Law goal?
c **Manchester United**

10 Now for Aberdeen's greatest achievement – winning the European Cup-Winners' Cup in 1983. Which mighty team did the Dons beat in the final?
a **Real Madrid**

11 In which Scandinavian city was the final played?
c **Gothenburg**

12 Can you name the stadium that staged the rain-drenched final?
a **Nya Ullevi**

13 Who was the manager this cup-winning side?
a **Alex Ferguson**

14 And who captained the team?
b **Willie Miller**

15 Who scored Aberdeen's winning goal?
b **John Hewitt**

16 The final score was 2–1. Who scored Aberdeen's other goal?
c **Eric Black**

17 And who scored the opposition's goal?
d **Juan Gómez González ('Juanito')**

18 Which team did the Dandies beat to secure their place in the final?
a **Waterschei**

19 Some more recent European escapades. Which team knocked Aberdeen out of Europe in the season 2002–03?
c **Hertha Berlin**

20 Which of the Dandies' players was sent off in the away leg against this team?
a **Eric Deloumeaux**

21 In the previous season, Aberdeen suffered a humiliating defeat in Europe against which team of part-timers?
a **Bohemians (Eire)**

22 Some historical stuff. The name
Pittodrie comes from Gaelic and means
what?
b Hill of Dung

23 The club was founded in 1903.
According to the records, what was the
exact date?
b 14 April

24 What was the name of the club's first
manager?
a Jimmy Philip

25 In which season did the team first
wear red tops?
d 1938–39

26 What colour of jerseys did the Dons
wear prior to that?
b Yellow and black vertical stripes

27 The colours of their jerseys gave rise
to what early nickname for the team?
c The Wasps

28 And in which year did they adopt the
current all-red strip?
a 1966

29 In the Scottish Cup in 1923, the Dons
notched up a record number of goals
scored in a single game. How many did
they score?
c 13

30 And which club was on the receiving
end of this torrent of goals?
d Peterhead

31 Until season 2003–04, he was still
doing the job he'd held for many, many
years. What is the name of this long-
serving kit man?
b Teddy Scott

32 Aberdeen's domestic record. In which
season did Aberdeen first win the First
Division title?
d 1954–55

33 And how many times in total did the
Pittodrie side win this title?
d Once

34 How many times have the Dons won
the Scottish Premier League
Championship?
c Three times

35 How many times has the team won the
Scottish Cup?
b Seven times

36 And for how many consecutive seasons
was this trophy Pittodrie bound?
**c Four (1981–82, 1982–83, 1983–84
and 1984–85)**

37 How many times has an Aberdeen
captain picked up the League Cup?
c Six times

38 Which team did Aberdeen beat to win
the European Super Cup?
d Hamburg

39 The record crowd at Pittodrie stands at
45,061. What was the occasion?
**c A Scottish Cup tie against Hearts,
season 1953–54**

40 The biggest attendance at any game
involving the Dons was at the 1937
Scottish Cup final against Celtic. What
was the size of this crowd?
a 146,422

41 Star stats. From which club was the exceptionally gifted Pittodrie favourite Zoltan Varga signed?

c **Hertha Berlin**

42 Who was the Dons' top scorer in season 1979–80?

d **Steve Archibald (with 21 goals)**

43 He was signed from Morton in 1969. Can you name the Aberdeen player who was to become affectionately known as 'The King'?

a **Joe Harper**

44 Nicknamed 'Cup-tie', who was Aberdeen's two-goal hero when they won the Scottish Cup in season 1969–70?

c **Derek McKay**

45 What's the name of Aberdeen's mascot?

b **Angus the Bull**

46 He made 91 starts for Scotland. His last appearance was in October 1998 in the European Championship qualifier against Estonia. Who is he?

c **Jim Leighton**

47 He appeared in a Scotland jersey 34 times – twice as captain. In 1971, this Aberdeen-born defender was sold to Manchester United. Can you name this superstar?

b **Martin Buchan**

48 What piece of kitchen equipment was done away with in a famous Pittodrie cost-cutting exercise?

d **A toaster**

49 Whose biography, entitled *The King*, was published in the autumn of 2003?

c **Denis Law's**

50 And, finally, Aberdeen beat Celtic 2–0 (YES!!!!!!!) at Pittodrie in December 2001. What did Dons fans throw at the Celtic players during this game?

c **Snowballs**

7 Food

1 What are hairy tatties?
a Mashed potatoes and salt fish

2 Traditionally, when would you serve bubbly jock?
c At Christmas

3 What is a howtowdie?
a A young chicken that's ready for the pot

4 What's a collop?
b A thin slice of meat

5 What's the English name for a sybae?
d A spring onion

6 What is skirlie usually served with?
a Cooked meat, especially roast chicken or mince

7 And what is the main ingredient of skirlie?
a Oatmeal

8 It's called skirlie because . . .?
b The noise it makes when it's cooking sounds like skirling bagpipes

9 What's a softie?
c A doughy bread roll

10 In the north-east, they're known as 'breed'. What's the more common name for this Scottish delicacy?
a Oatcakes

11 What's the name of the world-famous breed of north-east beef cattle?
c Aberdeen Angus

12 If you were 'gawn' brumullin", what would you be doing?
d Going to pick blackberries

13 What's a mealie pudding?
a A sausage-shaped serving of skirlie

14 And what's another name for a mealie pudding?
b A mealie Jimmy

15 What are stovies?
d Potatoes, onions and leftover meat cooked together

16 A long-standing city delicacy, what is potted hough?
c Cooked beef or pork from the shin served in jelly

17 What is bawd bree?
d Hare soup

18 And what about partan bree?
a Crab soup

19 What's a lucky tattie?
b A tattie-shaped spicy sweetie with a wee plastic toy embedded in it

20 And, if your tatties have gone through the bree, what's happened to them?
d They've been boiled too long and are all soggy

21 Coarse, medium, fine and pinhead are grades of what?
a Oatmeal

22 A buttery is also known as what?
c A rowie

23 Stappit heidies are . . .?
a Stuffed fish heads

24 What would you expect to get if you ordered cabbi claw?
b Salt cod served with eggs, potatoes and often parsley

25 Where would you go if you fancied a cappie wi' juicie?

d The icer (ice-cream van)

26 And what would you get if you asked for a cappie wi' juicy?

a An ice-cream cone with raspberry sauce

27 Cullen skink is . . .?

b A smoked fish soup that originated in a Buchan village

28 Mackie's is a favourite brand of north-east what?

c Ice cream

29 Grunny Marshall recommends bramble jam as a cure for what?

c Sore throats

30 What is a clootie dumpling?

c A spicy steamed dessert made with dried fruit

31 And what does 'clootie' mean?

a Cloth

32 What are the main ingredients of clapshot?

b Neeps and tatties

33 What is 'chuddie'?

b Chewing gum

34 Which fruits would you need if you were making cranachan?

a Raspberries

35 A sheep's pluck is an essential ingredient of haggis. Which part of the animal is the pluck?

d All of the above

36 And what are an animal's 'lights'?

b Its lungs

37 In the song, Ally Bally was greetin' for another bawbee to buy what?

a Coulter's candy

38 If you ordered clabbie dubhs, what would you be served with?

c Mussels

39 What would you use a spurtle for?

b Keeping your porridge lump-free – it's a wooden stirring stick

40 When is black bun traditionally eaten?

a New Year

41 In Ireland, a mixture of tatties and cabbage is called colcannan. What's it called in Scotland?

d Rumbledthumps

42 A chipper in Stonehaven is said to have been the first to offer which culinary delight?

b The deep-fried Mars bar

43 Which of these is an essential ingredient of Scotch broth?

c Pearl barley

44 How can you tell if your Scotch pie has onions in it?

a It would have two holes in the top instead of just one

45 And, traditionally, what meat is used in Scotch pies

d Mutton

46 Dean's of Huntly are world-renowned makers of what?

b Shortbread

47 Pannanich Wells on Deeside is famous
for what?
b Its spring water

48 What is brochan?
**c Gruel with honey and butter, often
served as a bedtime drink**

49 There's a farm just off the South
Deeside Road where some unusual
animals are reared for food. What are
they?
a Ostriches

50 What's a tappit hen?
**c A whisky decanter with a stopper in
the form of a cock's comb**

8 Education

1 In the past, what would north-east bairns have called their teachers?
c **Dominies**

2 When was Aberdeen's first university at Old Aberdeen founded?
a **1495**

3 What is its name?
b **King's College**

4 And who was its founder?
c **Bishop William Elphinstone**

5 If somebody 'got the scud' at school, what would have happened to them?
d **Been belted by the teacher**

6 Aberdeen's other university was founded in which year?
c **1593**

7 And what is its name?
a **Marischal College**

8 And who was the principal mover in getting the 'New Town' university off the ground?
d **George Keith**

9 The first chair of what, in the English-speaking world, was founded at King's College in 1497?
a **Medicine**

10 If the teacher told a member of the class to 'Wheesht!', what would they be asking them to do?
b **Stop talking**

11 Marischal College was built on the site of what?
b **A Franciscan friary**

12 Who was the architect of the Broad Street frontage of Marischal College?
a **A Marshall Mackenzie**

13 What's the name of the hall and tower in Marischal College?
b **Mitchell**

14 If you were sent home from school because you were 'flechie', what would be wrong with you?
d **You'd have fleas**

15 An act of parliament of which year decreed that the city's two universities should merge?
c **1858**

16 How many universities in total were there in England at that time?
c **Five**

17 When was Robert Gordon's Institute of Technology granted university status?
a **1992**

18 If you were accused of 'swicking', what would you have been doing?
a **Cheating in a test or exam**

19 What is the city's school of architecture called?
d **Scott Sutherland**

20 And can you name Aberdeen's school of art?
a **Gray's**

21 And what about the agricultural college to west of the city?
b **Craibstone**

22 If a pupil was practising their 'scrieving', what would they be doing?
a **Practising writing**

23 What's the city's main library called?
c **Aberdeen Central Library**

24 On which street would you find this library?
a **Rosemount Viaduct**

25 In days gone by, what would a teacher have used to inflict corporal punishment?
b **A tawse**

26 What was the name of the city's all-girls' senior secondary school?
b **Aberdeen High School for Girls**

27 What's the name of this school now?
d **Harlaw Academy**

28 And can you name this school's most famous former pupil?
a **Annie Lennox**

29 If you'd forgotten to take your 'dookers' to school, which lesson would you miss?
d **Swimming – they're swimming trunks**

30 What was Aberdeen's first purpose-built comprehensive school?
b **Hazlehead Academy**

31 When was this comprehensive school opened?
c **1970**

32 And pupils from which school were moved there?
a **Aberdeen Academy**

33 Who officially opened the new school?
c **The Queen**

34 If the teacher tells you off for 'fiking', what have you been doing?
c **Fidgeting**

35 People are trained to become what at Blairs College on the outskirts of Aberdeen?
d **Roman Catholic Priests**

36 What is the annual university Torcher?
a **A charity parade by city students**

37 If a pupil was 'ettling' to do something, what would they be doing?
a **Trying to do it**

38 What was the name of the school opposite Robert Gordon's College?
b **Aberdeen Academy**

39 What was this school called before 1954?
d **Central School**

40 Now called The Academy, what is housed in the old school today?
b **A shopping centre with restaurants**

41 If you were 'jouking the school', where would you be?
d **Any of the above – it means playing truant**

42 When King's College first opened, its main purpose was for training people in which two professions?
a **The Church and law**

43 Who became the first principal of King's College in 1514?
b **Hector Boece**

44 And, in 2003, who holds the post of principal of the University of Aberdeen?
a **Professor C Duncan Rice**

45 Who, in session 2003–04, is the rector of the University of Aberdeen?
b **Clarissa Dickson Wright**

46 If a class thought their teacher was 'fair stunkit', which of the following would they be?
a **In a bad mood**

47 What's the name of the main library of the University of Aberdeen?
c **The Queen Mother Library**

48 When King's College first opened, at what age did students normally begin their studies there?
a **Fourteen**

49 If a teacher gave a pupil an 'owergyann', what would it be?
c **A scolding**

50 What's the name of the University of Aberdeen's student newspaper?
d ***Gaudie***

9 Famous Folk

1 He took the first ever photos of the moon and was appointed Astronomer Royal in1879. Who is this Aberdeen-born astronomer?

a **Sir David Gill**

2 Which architect designed the city's Music Hall?

d **Archibald Simpson, John Smith and James Matthews collaboratively**

3 What's the real name of the self-styled Torry Quine?

a **June Imray**

4 Who's the MSP for Aberdeen North?

b **Elaine Thomson**

5 What's the name of the Aberdonian character in the BBC soap River City?

b **Roisin (pronounced Rosheen)**

6 And can you name the actor who plays her?

c **Joyce Falconer**

7 What's the name of the Aberdeen songstress who formed the band Eurythmics with Dave Stewart?

a **Annie Lennox**

8 What was the name of the previous band she was in?

c **The Tourists**

9 And what's the name of her most recent solo album?

b *Annie Lennox – Bare*

10 The author of *A Scots Quair*, which Scots novelist worked as a journalist on the *Aberdeen Journal* at the end of the First World War?

b **Lewis Grassic Gibbon**

11 Born at Gilcomston in the city in 1848, what's the name of Aberdeen's famous female missionary?

a **Mary Slessor**

12 Who is the MP for Aberdeen South?

c **Anne Begg**

13 Known as the father of Scottish Country Dancing, he opened the city's first dance school in the eighteenth century. Can you name him?

d **Francis Peacock**

14 What's the name of the poet who, in 1357, became archdeacon of St Machar's Cathedral?

c **John Barbour**

15 What's the name of the artist famous for his Aberdeen cityscapes?

b **Eric Auld**

16 The first Photographer Royal was an Aberdonian. Who was he?

c **George Washington Wilson**

17 Who is the MP for Aberdeen Central?

a **Frank Doran**

18 Born in Aberdeen in 1965, which profoundly deaf person became a world-famous percussionist and composer?

d **Evelyn Glennie**

19 Can you name the Aberdeen-born Olympic gold-medallist swimmer?

a **David Wilkie**

20 For which event did this person win their gold medal?

d The 200m breaststroke

21 And at which games did they win it

b Munich, 1972

22 He was most famous for playing Dr Cameron in *Dr Finlay's Casebook*. Who was this actor who was born in Aberdeen in 1907?

b Andrew Cruickshank

23 Born at Craigmyle, just outside the city, in 1814, what title did Sir Walter Scott bestow on magician John Henry Anderson?

a The Great Wizard of the North

24 Famous as one of 'The Goodies', he was born in Aberdeen in 1943. What's his name?

a Graeme Garden

25 Who's the MSP for Aberdeen Central?

d Lewis MacDonald

26 Educated at the University of Aberdeen, he became a Northsound DJ before heading for shows on Radio 1 and venturing into TV. Who is he?

c Nicky Campbell

27 Brought up in Kintore, can you name this choreographer and dancer who was born in Aberdeen in 1962?

a Michael Clark

28 What was the name of the first general manager of the BBC? He was born in Stonehaven in 1889.

b John Reith

29 One of Scotland's top businessmen, he's also chairman of Aberdeen FC. Who is he?

d Stewart Milne

30 Can you name the fiddler and composer of fiddle music, known as 'The Strathspey King', who was born at Banchory in 1843?

a James Scott Skinner

31 Who's the MSP for Aberdeen South?

a Nicol Stephen

32 He lived in Forres and was one half of the folk duo The Corries. Can you name him?

c Roy Williamson

33 And what is the name of the other member of The Corries?

d Ronnie Browne

34 Who is world champion squash player who was born in Inverurie in 1973?

b Peter Nicol

35 He was born in Aberdeen in 1888 and became a popular comic film actor. Who was he?

a Will Hay

36 Which Aberdeen-based golfer won the 1999 Open Golf Championship at Carnoustie?

d Paul Lawrie

37 Who's the MP for Aberdeen North?

d Malcolm Savage

38 Born in 1777 just outside Stonehaven, what was Robert Barclay Allardice famous for?

a Long distance walking

39 Which comedian, the self-styled 'Laird of Inversnecky', was born in the city in 1893?

c **Harry Gordon**

40 Which BBC Scotland sports presenter is an Aberdonian?

b **Richard Gordon**

41 Sir Ian Wood is Chairman and Chief Executive of the John Wood Group plc. He graduated with a first class honours degree in which subject?

a **Psychology**

42 What's the name of the famous poet who was born in the London but moved to the city shortly after his birth in 1788?

d **George Gordon**

43 How is this poet better known?

c **Lord Byron**

44 Lady Caroline Lamb famously described him as . . .?

b **Mad, bad and dangerous to know**

45 What's the name of the BBC news reporter who was raised in Aberdeen?

a **Eric Crockart**

46 Who was the Fraserburgh-born man who founded the Japanese shipbuilding firm that became Mitsubishi?

a **Thomas Blake Glover**

47 This man is believed to have been the model for a character in which Puccini opera?

b ***Madama Butterfly***

48 He was born in Ballater in 1854 and became known as the father of modern town-planning. Can you name him?

c **Sir Patrick Geddes**

49 Born in Braemar in 1945, can you name the folk singer who was one half of the duo Peter and Gordon?

d **Gordon Waller**

50 One of triplets, what's the name of the Aberdeen professional woman golfer?

a **Muriel Thomson**

10 Miscellaneous

1 One of Scotland's biggest prisons is in which north-east town?
d Peterhead

2 What's the name of Aberdeen's prison?
a Craiginches

3 Which of the city's statues was described as 'not a man in a chair but a chair with a man in it'?
c Prince Albert's

4 Which north-east town holds the annual Ythan Raft Race?
a Ellon

5 Where, in the north-east, is there a new-age commune?
d Findhorn

6 When was Scotland's oldest lighthouse built?
b 1787

7 And this lighthouse is in which north-east town?
c Fraserburgh

8 Originally, what fuelled the light of this lighthouse?
a Whale oil

9 The area around Inverurie is called the Garioch. How do you pronounce this?
d Gearay (as in gear ray)

10 Which town holds a Festival of Traditional Music and Song each June?
d Keith

11 Lossiemouth is the birthplace of which former prime minister?
c Ramsay MacDonald

12 Which north-east town is renowned for its marble?
b Portsoy

13 And marble from this town was used in the construction of which famous building?
c The Palace of Versailles

14 Who became manager of Aberdeen Football Club in May 1999?
a Ebbe Skovdahl

15 And who took over from him in December 2002?
d Steve Paterson

16 What's the name of the famous north-east trout fishery?
a Glen of Rothes

17 If you catch one of this fishery's tagged fish, what prize can you claim?
c A half bottle of malt whisky

18 One of the largest agricultural shows is held in which Aberdeenshire town?
d Turriff

19 According to the song, where does the floo-er o' a' the bonnie lasses bide?
b Fyvie-o

20 Where is the north-east's unofficial naturist beach?
a Balmedie

21 What's the name of the Hazlehead riding school?
d Hayfield

22 Which north-east town is home to Scotland's Lighthouse Museum?
a Fraserburgh

23 Where, in the city centre, would you go if you wanted a game of tenpin bowling?

c **George Street**

24 What's the name of the cartoon couple in the *Evening Express*?

a **Dod 'n' Bunty**

25 What's the Boddam Coo?

b **A foghorn**

26 Which former punk rocker wrote a book about stone circles, many of which are in Aberdeenshire?

d **Julian Cope**

27 What's the name of the children's theme park off the South Deeside Road?

a **Storybook Glen**

28 Which contemporary author claimed that magic was 'not living in Aberdeen anymore'?

b **Christopher Brookmyre**

29 What activity would you go to Glenshee or the Lecht for?

a **Winter sports**

30 Which of the city's golf courses holds an annual pro-cel-am tournament?

c **Deeside**

31 What's the small blue tower at the Holburn Street end of Justice Mill Lane for?

b **It's a ventilator for sewer gas**

32 Apart from a castle, what's a balmoral?

d **A brimless hat**

33 What's the name of the hands-on education centre Constitution Street?

a **Stratosphere**

34 What's the name of the model farm near Lumphanan?

a **Noah's Ark Model Farm**

35 Which north-east town hosts the Scottish Traditional Boat Festival in June each year?

b **Portsoy**

36 What's the name of AFC's internet supporters' football team?

c **Inter Ma Lamb**

37 What's the name of the Aberdeenshire road that's frequently closed because of heavy snow?

a **Cock Bridge to Tomintoul**

38 Which town is Deeside Gliding Club nearest to?

a **Aboyne**

39 What's the monument at the end of the North Pier in Fittie called?

d **Scarty's Monument**

40 And what is the purpose of the monument?

a **It's a vent for a sewer outlet**

41 What's the name of the farm at Nigg that specialises in rare breeds of sheep and cattle?

c **Doonies**

42 Which city church has the largest set of bells of any church in the Britain?

c **St Nicholas**

43 And how many bells does it have?
a 48

44 What's the name of Aberdeen's airport?
c Dyce

45 Which Shakespearean character is said
to have been killed at Lumphanan in
Aberdeenshire?
d Macbeth

46 In which Aberdeenshire village is there
a woollen mill museum?
b Garlogie

47 What's the name of the New-Pitsligo-
born fashion designer?
c Bill Gibb

48 What's a 'poor-oot'?
**a Money the father of a bride throws
to local bairns**

49 What's the name of the cliffs just north
of Cruden Bay?
d Bullers of Buchan

50 And what does 'bullers' mean?
a Rushing waters

HOW DID YOU DO?

Score Comment

401–500   Well done! You're a Doric-spikin', buttery-eatin', Dandies-supportin' chiel o' the first order – either that or you spent hours raking about on the internet, trying to find the right answers.

301–400   Nae bad! At least you know you've been insulted when someone calls you a feel gype.

201–300   Room for improvement! Awa' and hiv mince, tatties and skirlie for your supper before folk think you come from Scumdee.

101–200   You moved to Westhill from London how long ago?

0–100   So, have you enjoyed your short holiday in the city?